A Compact Guide to the Bible

Karen Lee-Thorp

NAVPRESS

A Compact Guide
to the Bible

Karen Lee-Thorp

NAVPRESS
BRINGING TRUTH TO LIFE
P.O. Box 35001, Colorado Springs, Colorado 80935

The Navigators is an international Christian organization. Our mission is to reach, disciple, and equip people to know Christ and to make Him known through successive generations. We envision multitudes of diverse people in the United States and every other nation who have a passionate love for Christ, live a lifestyle of sharing Christ's love, and multiply spiritual laborers among those without Christ.

NavPress is the publishing ministry of The Navigators. NavPress publications help believers learn biblical truth and apply what they learn to their lives and ministries. Our mission is to stimulate spiritual formation among our readers.

© 2001 by The Navigators
All rights reserved. No part of this publication may be reproduced in any form without written permission from NavPress, P.O. Box 35001, Colorado Springs, CO 80935. www.navpress.com
Library of Congress Catalog Card Number: 2001032975
ISBN 1-57683-255-4

Cover design by Ray Moore
Series Editor: Brad Lewis
Creative Team: Marla Kennedy, Terry Behimer, Glynese Northam

Unless otherwise identified, all Scripture quotations in this publication are taken from the HOLY BIBLE: NEW INTERNATIONAL VERSION® (NIV®). Copyright © 1973, 1978, 1984 by International Bible Society. Used by permission of Zondervan Publishing House. All rights reserved. Other versions used include: the *New American Standard Bible* (NASB), © The Lockman Foundation 1960, 1962, 1963, 1968, 1971, 1972, 197, 1975, 1977, 1995; *The Message: New Testament with Psalms and Proverbs* (MSG) by Eugene H. Peterson, copyright © 1993, 1994, 1995, used by permission of NavPress Publishing Group.

Lee-Thorp, Karen
 A compact guide to the Bible / Karen Lee-Thorp.
  p.cm.
 Includes bibliographical references.
 ISBN 1-56783-255-4
  1. Bible--Introductions. I. Title
BS475.2 .L39 2001
220.6'1--dc21   2001032975

Printed in the United States of America

1 2 3 4 5 6 7 8 9 10 / 05 04 03 02 01

Contents

A PLAN

Acknowledgments

This Compact Guide is a brief tour of its subject matter. For a deeper look, I recommend *The Language of God: A Commonsense Approach to Understanding and Applying the Bible* by David Crabtree, J.A. Crabtree, and Ron Julian; *Playing With Fire* by Walt Russell; *Reading the Bible with Heart and Mind* by Tremper Longman; *How to Read the Bible for All Its Worth* by Gordon Fee and Douglas Stuart; and *Hearing God* by Dallas Willard. I am indebted to all of these works (and others too numerous to list) for their wisdom on the Bible.

Why Do I Need This Book?

> *What you say goes, GOD,*
> *and stays, as permanent*
> *as the heavens.*
> *Your truth never*
> *goes out of fashion;*
> *it's as up-to-date as*
> *the earth when*
> *the sun comes up.*
> **Psalm 119:89-90**, MSG

You need this book if:

- You've started reading the Bible on your own, but at about the point where it says, "Anyone who curses his father or mother must be put to death" (Exodus 21:17), you've hit a wall. You wonder, "Does this apply to my family?"
- You've faced a difficult situation where you didn't know what to do. "What would Jesus do?" you asked yourself. Then you realized you had no idea what Jesus would do.
- You struggle with a habit like anger or anxiety. You've prayed for the Holy Spirit to help you overcome your habit, but so far not much has changed.
- You know some individual Bible verses, but there are vast portions that remain uncharted waters for you.
- You avoid reading the Bible, either because it seems like too much work or because it makes you feel bad about yourself.
- You're bewildered by people who read the Bible a lot but don't seem to show much benefit.

- You are often so caught up in the hassles of your own life that you lose sight of the bigger picture.

You need this book if:

- You want to know God.
- You want to see the world the way God does.
- You want to grow in your ability to hear God speaking to you.
- You want to be able to recognize good, fair, and poor Bible teaching.
- You want to understand and participate in the plan of God.
- You want a systematic but not boring path through God's Word.
- You want to be able to find answers to your big questions in the Bible.

You can browse this book as well as read it. The Table of Contents can steer you toward the particular question you'd like to address. You'll find **hyperlinks** that point you to other parts of the book that build on what you've been reading. Or, you can read straight through the book for the whole story.

The perspective of this book is based on a traditional evangelical statement of belief regarding the Bible:

> We believe the Scripture of the Old and New Testaments as inspired by God, and inerrant in the original writing, and that they are of supreme and final authority in faith and life.

(For more on **inspiration,** see page 46. For more on **authority,** see page 53.)

The Bible is the most important book you will ever read. If you learn how to get the most out of it, the rewards will astound you.

The Big Picture

A Christian is spiritual when he sees everything from God's viewpoint.

A. W. Tozer[1]

What Does the Bible Offer Me?

As the deer pants
for streams of water
so my soul
pants for you,
O God.

Psalm 42:1

Knowing God.

In these days when books are cheap and almost everyone can read, it's easy to take for granted that you have total access to the written words of the unseen Being who created the universe. But think about it.

The infinite God is unknowable except to the extent that He chooses to reveal Himself. He reveals Himself through the natural world: "The basic reality about God is plain enough. Open your eyes and there it is! By taking a long and thoughtful look at what God has created, people have always been able to see what their eyes as such can't see: eternal power, for instance, and the mystery of his divine being" (Romans 1:20 MSG). Stars and insects reflect His glory. He speaks in other ways too, but He has chosen to reveal Himself most clearly through the words and events recorded in the Bible. He has acted in history and inspired writers to record those acts for your benefit. He has spoken through prophets, and those prophets have written down His words to enlighten all generations.

What Is God Like?

- Is God a Person with a personality or an impersonal Force?
- What does God like and not like?
- What does God think is very important, sort of important, and not important at all?
- What makes Him mad?
- What makes Him sing?
- What makes Him laugh?
- If you disappoint Him, what is He most likely to do?
- If you're in trouble, what can you reasonably expect from Him?
- What was God doing four thousand years ago?
- What is He up to now?
- What are His ultimate goals for our planet?

The Bible offers you a chance to see how God has interacted with stubborn people, proud people, scared people, all kinds of people. Taken together, these records will give you a good reading on how God will interact with you when you are stubborn, scared, or whatever. Can you trust Him? Does He deserve your love, your unflagging allegiance, your worship? If you're mildly interested in God, the Bible can satisfy your curiosity. But if you're seriously considering centering your life on God's agenda, it's worth your while to check out that agenda thoroughly, read the fine print, and verify whether this God deserves such commitment. Otherwise, when believing in God costs you something, you will have second thoughts.

When times are tough, it's hard to have faith in someone unless you have a rich and accurate understanding of whom that person is. Is God utterly good? How do you know? Is God all-powerful? What's the evidence? How important to God is your individual little life? God will speak to you about these things through the Scriptures.

The chief emphasis in your Bible study should be to immerse yourself in who God is. The goal is not simply to understand God's attributes theoretically, but to fill your mind with this magnificent God so that you delight in your heavenly Father. Bible reading should inspire passionate love and awe of God—a passion that leads to fearlessness with regard to the things the world throws at you. All the stories and teachings of the Bible are given primarily to reveal this beautiful and astonishing God to the deepest levels of your intellect, emotions, and will.

Guidance in making wise decisions.

The Bible will not tell you whom to marry or whether to take the job that has just been offered to you. It will not tell you whom to vote for or which church to attend. However, it will help you become wise enough in the ways of God to make good decisions in those areas. (For more on **wisdom,** see page 157.) The Bible will describe the kind of person who would make a good mate and will give you plenty of examples of wise and unwise choices for partners. It will tell you how God views work. It will train you to recognize the qualities of a good political leader. It will show you what the church is for and how an effective church operates.

The Bible will help you become a spiritual adult when it comes to making decisions. A child doesn't know how to make wise decisions about things as important as marriage or voting. A child needs a parent to say, "No, you may not have ice cream for dinner. You will have chicken, rice, and carrots." The process of growing up is supposed to train a child to make wise decisions about alcohol, sex, entertainment, and what to eat for dinner. Then the 25-year-old need not phone her parents to ask what she should eat. God does not want you to be a robot, mindlessly taking orders at every turn. God wants you to be an adult, taking orders when He gives them and thinking for yourself when the situation calls for thinking.

This does not mean God will never give you specific instructions or counsel. It will always be appropriate to pray to your heavenly Parent for *specific* guidance. However, what God wants to say to you about the *general* principles that should guide your decision has already been written in the Bible.

In addition to being the Son of God and Savior of the World, Jesus is also the wisest teacher who ever lived. His teaching, recorded in the Gospels, is the wisest teaching available anywhere on how to live well. His life example, also recorded in the Gospels, is the finest model you could have for a life wisely lived.

A chance to learn about life from other people's mistakes.

Trial and error is one of the chief ways in which we learn. Watching other people's trials and errors speeds the process. Want to know what will probably happen if you try to make your life work by manipulating and deceiving others? You can do it for a few years and see what happens, but you can save yourself the agony if you read the story of Jacob in the book of Genesis. Similarly, the apostles made loads of dumb mistakes during their three years with Jesus. Why reinvent a broken wheel? Read all about it in the Gospels.

Help in becoming the kind of person you want to become.

The evidence that the Holy Spirit is active in your life is that you are becoming increasingly loving, joyful, peaceful, patient when things go wrong, ethical, kind, able to deal with wrongdoers effectively without lashing back, and free of destructive habits (Galatians 5:22-23). One of the Spirit's main tools for accomplishing this is the Bible. You can listen to the Word being read or recited, and you can benefit from great teachers. But if you really want to become as loving, joyful, peaceful, etc. as you are capable of being, read the Scriptures both on your own and in a worshiping community. (For more on **transformation,** see page 63.)

Accurate eyeglasses through which to see the world clearly.

Everyone sees the world through a pair of eyeglasses, a set of basic assumptions. These assumptions tell you how to interpret what you experience. Your assumptions are called your *worldview*.

Your worldview is made up of your answers to basic questions.

For example, the Western worldview today is extremely individualistic. Westerners (most people in Europe and North America) believe that a person comes up with his or her own identity as an individual. This is quite different from finding your identity through your ethnic group, your family, or your spiritual community. The Western worldview says your main goal in life is to find meaning and purpose for your individual life. Personal fulfillment and individual satisfaction is the target. Finding your identity is an individual quest. If you don't find meaning and purpose for yourself, no one can do it for you. Your family, the church, work, hobbies, and friends are all part of a giant buffet from which you can select items to assemble a life that gives you meaning. (For more on the **Western worldview,** see page 38.)

Worldview Questions

- Is there a God?
- If so, what is He/It like?
- How do I fit into the world—what is my purpose in life?
- Can science help me know the world as it really is?
- Are humans basically good or basically evil?
- How do I determine whether a choice is right or wrong?
- What happens when I die?
- What is the root cause of suffering?
- From where do I get my identity?

> Our basic criterion for doing or not doing something is whether it has potential to satisfy or fulfill us as an individual and give our life meaning and purpose.[2]

Once your worldview is formed, it's hard to change. Experience alone rarely challenges it because you interpret your experience so as to fit into your worldview. One of the great functions of the Bible is to free you from the worldview you have adopted from your culture and help you to see the world through God's eyes.

Do not conform any longer to the pattern of this world, but be transformed by the renewing of your mind. Then you will be able to test and approve what God's will is—his good, pleasing and perfect will. (Romans 12:2)

The more you allow the Scriptures, worship, and prayer to renew your mind, the more you will see things from God's point of view. It will become clear why His will—His commandments and priorities—is good, pleasing, and perfect. The Bible can show you not only what God wants you to do, but also *why* this is the wise and loving course of action. You'll see what God thinks is important and why. You'll be able to look at the most painful experience and, even when you don't know the specific *why* for this event, you'll see it not as a random occurrence in an aimless world, nor as the cruel act of a heartless God, but as part of a large plan of a good God.

Any doubt on this point gives force to the soul-numbing idea that God's commandments are, after all, only for his benefit and enjoyment, and that in the final analysis we must look after ourselves.[3]

The Biblical Worldview

- What God has done for you in Christ puts to rest all doubts about His love for you.
- Your identity comes from what Christ has done for you and in you.
- You are a player in a huge drama that is far bigger and more important than your personal worries.
- Meaning, purpose, and satisfaction come from aligning your life with the plan God has been working out in history for thousands of years.
- No player in the drama is insignificant.
- God's plan for the world is more important than an individual's feelings of personal fulfillment.

- You can find meaning and purpose only by teaming up with the rest of God's people. There are no Lone Ranger disciples.
- If you align yourself with God's plan, the benefits to you and to the world far outweigh the costs.
- God is so beautiful and amazing that He deserves whatever He asks of you.

Right now, some aspects of God's worldview may disturb you. A God who doesn't put your feelings first may seem like a God you don't want. Only when you immerse yourself in God's point of view on your individual life and on history will you be able to break free from the automatic question, "What's in it for me?" Only when you drink in the magnificence of God, the wonder of His kingdom, and the glory of His plan will you be able to believe, deep down, that this God and this kingdom are worth your love and commitment. Until you are captivated by God's beauty, you will always put yourself first. That's where the Bible can help you—by showing you a God worth living for, sacrificing for, even dying for.

A role in an epic drama that is far bigger than your life.

The great Story that runs through the Bible is God's relentless pursuit of those whom He loves. In the early chapters of Genesis, He created humans to be His family, but they rejected Him. The rest of the Bible recounts His daring plan to free them from the consequences of their folly and bring them home. Each human character in the drama—no matter how crucial his or her role is—must play it out with only limited knowledge of what his or her life ultimately contributes to the whole. Thus, Abraham is promised countless descendants but lives to see only two.

So much of life is minutia: getting dressed, fighting traffic, accomplishing tasks and errands, paying bills. The Scriptures invite you to see your life story as part of a much larger Story. Jesus calls His disciples "friends." The apostle Paul calls his friends "partners in the gospel." Through the Bible, God summons you to be a friend and partner with people across town and with those separated from you by oceans and centuries—all committed to the unfolding drama under the great Director.

A means through which God can talk to you personally.

The Bible is not a Ouija board. It is possible to misuse the Bible and deceive yourself about what God is saying. (For more on **sound interpretation,** see page 81.) Nevertheless, God does want to talk to you personally, and one of His preferred ways of doing this is through the Bible. If you memorize Scripture, you give Him the opportunity to raise a passage to your conscious awareness when you need it. (For more on **hearing God through the Scriptures,** see pages 69-74.) If you read the Bible regularly, you increase the likelihood of encountering a passage that speaks to your situation. The more biblical material you have stored in your brain, the more God has available to use. Yes, He can use other material stored in your brain—old song lyrics, childhood memories, a street sign. He can even talk to you through a donkey (Numbers 22:21-41). But He likes to use the words of the Bible.

Also, the more familiar you are with the biblical worldview, the more able you will be to discern when something that seems like the voice of God isn't God. God never contradicts what He has said in Scripture.

Training in love.

"Knowledge puffs up, but love builds up" (1 Corinthians 8:1). Knowing all the right doctrine and the whole history of Israel is worse than useless if it doesn't help you love God and others well.

> *"'Love the Lord your God with all your heart and with all your soul and with all your mind.' This is the first and greatest commandment. And the second is like it: 'Love your neighbor as yourself.' All the Law and the Prophets hang on these two commandments."* (Matthew 22:37-40)

If you study the Bible in order to be right and win debates, you will drain the Scriptures of their power in your life. But if you approach them with a humble desire to see God and grow in love, the results will amaze you.

What's the Bible About?

Every part of Scripture is God-breathed and useful one way or another — showing us truth, exposing our rebellion, correcting our mistakes, training us to live God's way. Through the Word we are put together and shaped up for the tasks God has for us.

2 Timothy 3:16-17, MSG

God.

First and foremost, the Bible is about God. It is God's account of His activities to create and redeem humans and the rest of planet Earth. The opening chapters of Genesis are not primarily about physics or biology, but about the Creator. Genesis 12-50 is not primarily about Abraham, Isaac, Jacob, and Joseph.[4] It's about how God intervened in history to set His plan in motion. God is always the Hero of the story, and the human characters play supporting roles.

The section of the Bible called the Law is about God's justice, holiness, standards of right and wrong, concern for the poor and vulnerable, and hatred of sin and evil. The Law is about God setting up a covenant or agreement about the relationship between Himself as Deliverer and King, and His chosen people as grateful subjects. (For more on **Law and covenant,** see page 144.)

The books of the Prophets are about how God responded when His people broke their end of the covenant. The New Testament is about how God dealt once and for all with sin and death, and how He formed a new covenant people to carry His plan to completion. The New Testament reveals God acting as Father, Son, and

Holy Spirit to accomplish God's purposes. Throughout the entire Bible, the focus is always on God.

Therefore, whenever you read a passage of Scripture, your first question should be about God. Don't leap right away to humans—especially yourself. There are thousands of books that can help you understand yourself. There are very few that can help you know God. The Bible is at the very top of that shorter list.

Questions About God

- What does this passage reveal about God's nature?
- What does it tell me about God's priorities?
- What does God say here?
- What does God do?
- How does God respond to human behavior here?
- What is my life like because God is like this?
- How will I speak and act because this is true?
- How can I come to really believe that God has done for me what this passage says?

God's plan.

From before the moment when God first created matter and energy out of nothing, God has had a plan for this universe: "to bring all things in heaven and on earth together under one head, even Christ" (Ephesians 1:10). As Christians, His plan means that no matter what confusion life throws at us and no matter what about the world doesn't make sense to us, we can look forward to the time when everything will make sense under the headship of Jesus Christ. In Genesis God planted the seeds of His plan, and in Revelation He brings it to flower. Each time you read a chapter of the Bible, ask how the events or teaching there contribute to your understanding of God's plan.

For example, the story of David and Goliath is only secondarily about David's faith. It's primarily about how God (the Hero of the story) chose a champion whose heart was so devoted to God's plan that he became a key player in the plan. If you read 1 Samuel 17 you'll see how God's plan was consistently at the front of David's mind, while the other Israelites were focused on their personal survival. You can read the Gospels or the New Testament letters with the same question in mind: "What does this tell me about God's plan?"

Questions About God's Plan

- How does this passage help me understand God's plan?
- What can I learn from this passage about the plan of salvation?
- How do the events of this chapter contribute to God's overall plan?
- What is Paul saying here about God's plan?
- What is my life like because this is true?
- How can I participate in God's plan today?

God's plan includes His strategy to save humans from sin and death by grace through faith in Jesus Christ. It explains what "save," "grace," and "faith" mean, and it helps us comprehend the ravages of sin and death. So God's plan is not some lofty vision for the universe far removed from your day-to-day life. What God did through Christ—and continues to do—makes all the difference for your ability *this minute* to have the Holy Spirit working in your life. And it makes all the difference for what you can expect when you die.

Still, if you think God's plan is only about personal salvation, the Bible can broaden your horizon. The entire universe—the earth, the angels, everything— waits eagerly for the culmination of that plan (Romans 8:18-22).

Jesus Christ.

God is three Persons—Father, Son, and Spirit—in one united God. It is God the Father that is most apparent in the Old Testament, but there are hints of Christ throughout those books. Much of the Old Testament is about God preparing a people with the background necessary to understand who Christ was going to be and what He was going to do.

The four Gospels are thoroughly about Jesus. They were written chiefly to demonstrate that Jesus was indeed the promised Messiah or Christ. The events were recorded to draw people to become disciples or followers of Jesus, and to help bring such disciples to maturity. Jesus' teaching explains who a disciple is and how he or she lives. Jesus' life also models how a disciple lives. Jesus' trial and crucifixion—which take up a large section of each Gospel—show the Messiah being executed on our behalf in order to free us from sin and death. His resurrection is the proof that He is who He claims to be. Thus, the Gospels are only secondarily about the faith or faithlessness of the disciples and others. They are primarily about Jesus.

Likewise, the New Testament letters also focus on Christ. Paul spends at least half of each letter describing how Christ works out the plan of God. Only then does he discuss how you should live in light of what God has done through Christ. (For more on **Jesus in the Gospels,** see page 169.)

Questions About Jesus

- How does this Old Testament prophecy point toward Christ?
- How does this gospel story show Jesus acting as the Messiah?
- What does this story reveal about Jesus' character?
- What does it tell me about His priorities?
- What were the habits by which Jesus sustained His intimacy with the Father?

- What does Jesus teach me to do here?
- What does Jesus ask me to believe?
- What does Paul say about Jesus here?
- How will this insight about Jesus affect the way I speak and act?

The Holy Spirit.

Jesus compares the Spirit to wind: We see the results of His actions rather than the Spirit Himself (John 3:8). In the Old Testament, the Holy Spirit is the One who inspires the speech and miracles of the Prophets. In the Gospels, Jesus speaks and works by the power of the Holy Spirit (Luke 4:14). The book of Acts could be called the Acts of the Holy Spirit, for it is the Spirit who empowers the apostles' words and deeds. When we say the Scriptures are inspired or "God-breathed" (2 Timothy 3:16), we are referring to God breathing His Spirit into the writers of Scripture. Note the link between the words "Spirit" and "inspire." (For more on **inspiration,** see page 46.)

Questions About the Holy Spirit

- Where is the Holy Spirit at work in this passage?
- What can this passage tell me about the Spirit?
- What does the Spirit want to do in me? Through me?
- What is my life like because the Spirit is in it?
- How can I cooperate with the Spirit in my daily life?

The kingdom of God.

The Greek word *Christos* (Christ) and the Hebrew word *mashiach* (Messiah) both mean "Anointed One." It was a Hebrew custom to anoint new kings with oil; hence, Messiah and Christ simply mean King. God is the King of the universe, but humans have rebelled against His rule. God's plan is to bring the whole universe under the headship of Christ the King.

You can trace this theme throughout the Bible. In the Law, God gathers a nation under His leadership. He declares laws. Like the Near Eastern sheiks of that day, He inhabits a royal tent called the tabernacle. Later, God has a palace called the temple, but when the nation persists in its rebellion, the King departs (Ezekiel 10) and leaves the nation and the temple to be destroyed. For five centuries the people wait for God to restore the kingdom. They expect the Messiah to be a descendant of the last human king in the lineage of David. They do not expect God to come in the flesh. But then Jesus arrives, showing in both words and deeds that He is both son of David and Son of God. His constant message is, "The time is fulfilled, and the kingdom of God is at hand" (Mark 1:15, NASB). His parables and other teachings deal with the surprising nature of the kingdom and how the King expects people to respond. His authority over sin, sickness, evil spirits, the forces of nature, and even death displays His royal identity.

All of this is covered by Paul and the other New Testament writers. They explain what it means for us to live in the "in-between" time when God's kingdom has arrived in part, but has not yet come in its fullness. The kingdom is already-but-not-yet as we await the return of the King. The book of Revelation depicts that final return and the kingdom's glory. (For more on the **kingdom in the Gospels,** see page 172.)

Our culture is highly suspicious of authority figures, especially kings. We believe in democracy and mistrust unelected leaders. In *The Amber Spyglass*, bestselling novelist Phillip Pullman has actually proposed that the kingdom of heaven be replaced by the Republic of Heaven.[5] But the Bible maintains that God made the universe and keeps it going. Without God holding it together, the whole universe would fly apart (Colossians 1:16-17). Furthermore, He alone keeps evil from consuming the universe. For all these reasons, He has the right to be King.

Questions About the Kingdom

- How does the Father or Jesus display Himself as King in this passage?
- According to this passage, what is highly valued in the kingdom?
- What is less valued?
- What are the principles by which the kingdom runs?
- How does God respond to those who reject His right to be King?
- How does God respond to those who accept His right to be King?
- In what ways is the kingdom all around me right now?
- In what ways is the kingdom still to come?
- How do the citizens of the kingdom live?
- What is the mission of a kingdom citizen in this in-between time?
- What is my life like because of the kingdom?
- How can I speak and act as a kingdom citizen?

Israel.

Most of the Old Testament is about God's dealings with a group of people defined by their ethnicity. They are the biological descendants of Abraham, his son Isaac, and Isaac's son Jacob (who received the name Israel in midlife). People of other ethnicities intermarry with the Israelites, but the ethnic identity remains strong.

In the books of Exodus through Deuteronomy, God gives a set of laws roughly comparable to a constitution for Israel as a nation. In the book of Joshua, the nation begins to occupy a piece of real estate that is variously called the Promised Land, the Holy Land, Canaan, Israel, and Palestine. The land of Israel and the ethnic nation of Israel are closely linked. One central purpose of the Law is to draw clear boundaries between Israel and its pagan neighbors so that the nation can maintain its identity.

God cares about this clear national identity because He intends to make Israel the cornerstone of His plan to redeem all the nations of the earth (Genesis 12:1-3).

In the New Testament, the army of the pagan Romans controls the land of Israel. Only a remnant of the Israelite people still lives in the land. Others are scattered throughout the Roman Empire and beyond. By this time, the people of Israel are also called the Jews (from the tribe of Judah). A crisis comes when the Jewish Messiah arrives and is rejected by most Jews. This rejection puts ethnic Israelites in a complicated position regarding the kingdom and its King. The place of Jews and non-Jews in the kingdom of God becomes a subject of much discussion in the New Testament.

Questions About Israel

- What does this passage say about the life God intended for Israel?
- What does it say about Israel's mission in the world?
- What does Israel do in this passage?
- How does God respond to Israel here?
- What does God do about Israel's rebellion?
- What does Jesus say about Israel?
- What happens to Israel in the decades after the Resurrection?
- What relevance does this promise of God to Israel have for me?
- In what ways am I like Israel depicted here?
- In what ways is the church today like Israel depicted here?
- In what ways is it different?
- What does it say about God that He planned to work through one ethnic group to save all ethnic groups?

So why should you care that most of the Old Testament is addressed to an ethnic group called Israel? Because *very often God made commands or promises in the Old Testament that applied mainly or only to Israel,* not to you as a New Testament believer. For example:

Command:

"Anyone who curses his father or mother must be put to death." (Exodus 21:17)

Promise:

> "For your sake I will send to Babylon
> and bring down as fugitives all the Babylonians,
> in the ships in which they took pride." (Isaiah 43:14)

Why should you bother reading commands that don't apply to you? And how can you tell which commands apply to you and which don't? The fact is, you can learn a lot about God from the Law He gave Israel. (For more on **the Law,** see page 143.)

And why bother reading promises that were made to someone else? What could God possibly say to you through those? A great deal, in fact. Often the promises have significance for you even when they were given to someone else. They can tell you much about how God operates. But you need to be careful when you "claim" promises that were originally mailed to someone else's address. (For more on **promises,** see page 39.)

The church.

Israel is the focus of God's plan in the Old Testament. But in the Gospels and Acts, most members of ethnic Israel reject Jesus as Messiah. Paradoxically, many non-Jews accept Him. This sets up a situation that at first perplexes the apostles. Then Peter and Paul figure out what God is up to. God has thrown open the doors of the kingdom to anyone who will bow the knee to Jesus, regardless of ethnicity. It's no longer necessary to undergo rites that mark a person as a Jew in order to enter the kingdom.

The New Testament name for the community of those who are following Jesus is the *ekklesia.* This Greek word means "those who are called out" and is normally translated "the church." It doesn't refer to buildings—the earliest communities met in homes. The organizational structure evolved slowly over generations; in the beginning it was a loose international network of cell groups, mainly in urban centers.

Most of the New Testament letters are written to churches—communities of believers gathered in a locality. A few are written to individuals. Most of the letters are about what the church is and how it's supposed to function. When you read instructions to "you" in the letters, they are usually instructions about how you *plural* (the church) are supposed to relate to each other and to outsiders. It's impossible to do most of the things Jesus and Paul command without a community. The instructions are designed for a team, a community of people sharing life as partners in God's great enterprise. (For more on **what you can learn from the letters,** see page 179.)

Questions About the Church

- What can I learn from this passage about the church?
- What is the church's mission in the world?
- How does God want us to relate to each other?
- What common problem in the church does this passage address?
- What can I learn about my individual identity from what Paul says here about the church?
- What would it take for me to relate to a community in this way?

What is yet to come.

Much of the Bible is about the past (the history of how God has been working out His plan), and much is about the present (the availability of salvation, the Holy

Spirit's ongoing work in your heart, the spread of the kingdom, the church's task in the world). Yet the Scriptures also encourage you with assurance about the future.

God gives you just enough information about the future to equip you for the present. For example, you can know that life is not a repetitive cycle of death and rebirth, as those who believe in reincarnation assert. Nor is history wandering aimlessly. Instead, God tells you that history and your own life are moving toward a planned goal and that you have just one lifetime in which to play your part in the drama. God's promises about the future can free you from:

- meaninglessness
- fear about what will happen to you
- despair about the injustice in the world
- deceptive personal goals, such as fame or wealth

The Prophets, Jesus, and Paul all provide insight on what is yet to come. And the book of Revelation gives a breathtaking vision of the last things designed to strengthen believers here and now. (For more on **Revelation,** see page 185.)

Questions About What Is Yet to Come

- What does this passage say about the end toward which God is leading history?
- What can this passage tell me about eternity?
- What will happen to those who reject Christ?
- In light of what this passage tells me about the future, what does that say about God's present view of power, money, and fame?
- What is a wise way of preparing now for the future?
- What do God's promises about the future reveal about God Himself?
- What do I personally have to look forward to?
- How does this passage help me deal with present suffering?
- How will I speak and act now in light of what is to come?

You.

Finally, the Bible is about you. You can learn a tremendous amount about who you are, where you fit into the great plan, and how God wants you to lead your life. In a sense, you were there as a slave in Egypt, and God rescued you (the book of Exodus). You were there among the people who acted as though God was not their King and committed terrible atrocities because "everyone did as he saw fit" (Judges 21:25). You were there at the Cross mocking Jesus, and you were there weeping and embracing Him when He rose from the grave. In a sense, the whole story is about a loving God pursuing you.

Nevertheless, you will learn the most about you when you discipline yourself to look first for God, His plan, and His people. Because humans are naturally self-centered, it's natural to read the Bible for what it can tell you about you. Also, under the worldview of our culture, God, the Bible, and the church exist for the purpose of making *your* life meaningful and fulfilling. (For more on **worldview,** see page 21.) God's job is to give you "abundant life"—and "abundant" is culturally defined as happy and full of feelings of achievement. Under this assumption, the Bible's purpose is to show you how to lead a happy and fulfilling life. It's no surprise, then, that people visit a new church or open the Bible with the question, "What's in it for me?" The idea that you and the Bible and the church exist for God's purposes is foreign to our culture's thinking.

Nevertheless, it is so. You and the Bible exist for God. Luckily, God is not an egotist, an insane dictator, or a control freak. His plan includes your eternal joy as the most unique and beautiful human being you can be. In Christ's life, death, and resurrection, God has shown that you exist for the sake of a God who loves you passionately and will go to any length for your sake.

Still, if you come to the Bible with a narcissistic worldview, you will misread everything. Narcissism is self-centeredness. It's like Bette Midler's character in the film *Beaches*: "But enough about me. Let's talk about you. What do you think—about me?" Narcissism can keep you from seeing and fulfilling the role God has for you in His plan. While you're focused on your personal comfort and interests, you can squander your chance to be a player on God's stage.

Questions About You

- How am I like Israel, or Abraham, or the Corinthians in this passage?
- What does this passage tell me about who I am and what my life is like?
- What does this passage tell me about my future?
- How do my values compare to Jesus' values here?
- How can I deal with my current suffering with the attitude portrayed here?
- Deep down, do I believe this?
- God, please help me believe this is true!

To understand how confused you'll be if you think of yourself first, consider this verse from Jeremiah:

> *"For I know the plans I have for you," declares the LORD, "plans to prosper you and not to harm you, plans to give you a hope and a future."* (Jeremiah 29:11)

What a wonderful promise! You may want to claim this promise for yourself. But who is "you" in this verse? Does "you" refer to you? Actually, no. The prophecy begins back in verse 4: "This is what the LORD Almighty, the God of Israel, says *to all those I carried into exile from Jerusalem to Babylon*" (emphasis added). The "you" in this prophecy is plural: They are the ethnic Israelites or Jews driven from the Holy Land by the Babylonians. Here's a bigger chunk:

> *This is what the LORD says: "When seventy years are completed for Babylon, I will come to you [the exiled Jews] and fulfill my gracious promise to bring you back to this place [the land of Israel]. For I know the plans I have for you," declares the LORD, "plans to prosper you and not to harm you, plans to give you a hope and a future."* (Jeremiah 29:10-11)

In this passage, God promises "a hope and a future" to ethnic Israel. The individuals listening to Jeremiah are going to go into exile and will never see their homeland again. God makes no guarantes about their personal affluence in Babylon (although He gives some consolation in verses 5-7). He does not address their individual futures. He wants them to place their hope on the fact that in seventy years, when they themselves are dead, their children and grandchildren will have an opportunity to rebuild the nation. Their faith and hope must rest not on their individual futures, but on the assurance that God's plan is still moving forward, that God's kingdom is still on the horizon.

Now here's where you come in. Don't claim this promise unless you're prepared for God to fulfill it seventy years from now. But you can allow it to help you see past yourself into the larger plan.

What does this passage tell you about God? It says He is Lord of history, so even the most catastrophic event that could befall your nation cannot thwart His plan. Indeed, He can weave it into His plan. He loves His people enough to allow them to suffer some of the consequences of their rebellion: They will spend the rest of their lives in a foreign country. But even so, He gives them reason to hope. While He makes no promises that every individual will have a home and a family, He does tell them as a group to "Build houses. . . plant gardens. . . marry. . . increase in number" (Jeremiah 29:5-6). He is a God who cares for His people even when He lets them endure the consequences of their choices. Nevertheless, He wants His people to understand that their future and hope lie in His plan, not in their personal health or wealth. Their identity and meaning come from being part of His kingdom, not from what they do for a living, how much money they make, how many children they have, or anything else about them individually.

Exercise

Read all of Jeremiah 29. What does God say here *to Israel?* What do you learn about God—His nature, values, and way of going about things? If God is still the same God, with the same nature and values, what significance does this passage have for the church today? For you as an individual?

God is still the same. Therefore, whether you marry or not, whether you have children or not, whether you are rich or poor, no matter where you live, your life has meaning if you ally yourself with God, put your hope in His kingdom, and find your identity as a player in His plan. The fruit of your labor may not come for seventy years, when you are long gone to heaven. But you can have confidence that it will come.

This passage hits our culture's worldview, with its short-term perspective, square in the jaw. Is *anything* worth your time and energy if you may not see the results in your lifetime? Can you imagine "hope" that is focused not on what God will do for you personally in the next year, but on what God will do through you for the world over the next century? Certainly Jesus may return at any moment, but this passage challenges the impatience that insists He must hurry. Yes, Jeremiah 29 is about you. But see how much more you learn about you when you slow down to get the bigger picture?

I'm just trying to get through life day to day. I don't have the energy to get excited by God's plan for history. Is the Bible irrelevant for me?

You're not alone. Thousands of Christians are in survival mode. Life can fill our plates, whether with school, work, family, health, or a hundred other essentials. The God of the Bible is eager to meet you where you are. You may want to put the hard stuff (Prophets, historical books, etc.) on a side burner and make a priority of passages that help you know God intimately. You may want to focus on soaking deeply in a few key, brief passages. For example, you could spend a month coming to believe—deep in your gut—the truths of Psalm 23: "The LORD is my shepherd, I shall not be in want."

You may benefit from learning how to meditate on a passage of Scripture and how to pray through a passage. (For more on **meditation** and **praying through a passage,** see pages 71 and 73.)

In this episode of your life with the Bible, your goal may be to come to know and trust God in a way that enables you to relax and move beyond survival mode, even when events in your world are crazy.

Certain principles are in the

Bible because they are true. They are true and

helpful for all people, regardless of whether they

accept or reject the Bible's central claim.

Tom Minnery[1]

Is the Bible Reliable?

The revelation of GOD is whole
and pulls our lives together.
The signposts of GOD are clear
and point out the right road.
The life-maps of GOD are right,
showing the way to joy.
The directions of GOD are plain
and easy on the eyes.

Psalm 19:7-9, MSG

Who wrote the Bible?

The Koran was written by one person: Mohammed. *The Book of Mormon* was written by one person: Joseph Smith. By contrast, the Bible was written by several dozen different people between about 1400 B.C. and 100 A.D.[2] The writers of the Old Testament were mainly priests and prophets, although they didn't all make their livings through religious work (Amos, for example, was in agriculture). Their writings were collected over a span of a thousand years, yet they hang together remarkably well. The writers of the New Testament were apostles or people whose sources of information were apostles. They wrote within a span of about fifty years.

When you're reading a book in the Bible, it's helpful to know who wrote it, approximately when, and under what circumstances. Was it a time of relative peace and prosperity, or were

> Most of the biblical books were written "within four distinct periods of history: the time of Moses, the rule of David and Solomon, the time surrounding the exile to Babylon, and the time right after Jesus' death and resurrection."[3]

times hard? Was this prophet living in Israel or exiled in Babylon? Was this gospel writer a Jew or a Gentile? Good commentaries, some study Bibles, Bible dictionaries, and books with names like *Introduction to the Old Testament* can give you this information. (For more on **background sources,** see page 105.)

What does "inspiration" mean?

Inspired means "God-breathed" (2 Timothy 3:16). Inspiration is the process through which God guided the biblical writers to say exactly what He wanted them to say.

> Frequently when we think of inspiration, we conceive of something akin to the dictation theory: God revealed his words to the biblical author who wrote them down. In its most extreme version, the human author recorded word-for-word what God dictated. This understanding of inspiration leaves the human author's mind partially engaged, at most, with the content of what he was writing. Paul could have been daydreaming about sunbathing on the Adriatic beaches when he penned the book of Romans.[4]

Some of the Prophets do seem to have been writing or speaking at God's dictation, as they prefaced these prophecies with, "This is what the LORD says" (Isaiah 48:17). However, we have much evidence that for the most part, rather than dictating to the human writers, God worked within their individual personalities. For example, writing styles vary widely among the books. John was a fisherman—he wrote in simple Greek with a limited vocabulary. Luke wrote in much more educated Greek. Also, Paul's letters are full of his own personal comments and greetings. "Third and most significant, the books of the Bible claim to be the product of the human authors: Peter refers to Paul's letters; Jesus refers to the writings of Moses and Isaiah; Paul refers to the writings of the Prophets. In every case the books of the Bible are considered the works of the human authors."[5]

The books of the Bible are the authoritative Word of God not because God dictated them word-for-word but because God constructed "the personality, personal experience, and circumstances of each biblical author in such a way that each author wrote exactly what God wanted him to write. In other words, God authored the lives of each of the biblical writers. . . . In this way the individual books could reflect the personality of the human author while containing exactly what God wanted" written.[6] Further, the Holy Spirit was present and active in the writers, guiding their work without controlling their minds. God never treats anyone—not the biblical writers and not you—like mindless robots.

Sometimes a biblical writer sat down and worked on a book from start to finish. "At other times, a Bible book (such as Jeremiah) was the product of a long ministry and came into existence in various stages. Still other writers drew upon available sources (from a king's historical records, for example)."[7] The Holy Spirit was actively engaged in guiding each writer's process of gathering information or living out his lifetime of prophetic ministry.

> No prophecy of Scripture is a matter of one's own interpretation, for no prophecy was ever made by an act of human will, but men moved by the Holy Spirit spoke from God. (2 Peter 1:20-21, NASB)

What qualifies a book to be part of the Bible?

The term *canon* literally means a builder's rule, something to measure by. We call a body of authoritative literature a canon. The canon of Scripture is *"the standard for faith and practice* for God's people through the ages."[8]

By the time of Christ, Jews in Palestine agreed firmly about the canon of the Old Testament. The canon closed with the book of Malachi, written in the fourth century B.C. The books of the Old Testament used by Protestants correspond to the books Jesus knew as Scripture.

Protestants and Catholics disagree about how much authority they give to fifteen books that Protestants call the Apocrypha (which means "the hidden writings") and Catholics call deuterocanonical (which means "the second canon"). These are Jewish writings written after Malachi died and before Christ came. At the time of Christ, they were included in the Old Testament used by Greek-speaking Jews in Egypt but not by Hebrew-speaking Jews in Palestine. Protestants regard these books as partially informative about Jewish history, as well as devotionally interesting, but they put these books in the same category as books you might buy at your Christian bookstore: interesting but not divinely inspired. Roman Catholics include these books in their Bibles.[9]

They recognized the Holy Spirit's voice in those books.

The early church recognized the authority of the books in our New Testament based on three criteria:

- An apostle or several apostles were the source of the book's information.
- The book presented the truth about God and Jesus, in agreement with the Old Testament and eyewitness testimony from the apostles.
- The book was widely accepted throughout the church—not just by a splinter group—as the Word of God.

In the fourth century A.D., councils of church leaders met to make the canon official. These councils did *not* invest the canonical books with authority. Rather, they recognized what the vast majority of the church on three continents already agreed upon. They knew inspiration when they saw it. They recognized the Holy Spirit's voice in those books.

If we compare the books these councils embraced to the ones they rejected, we can see that their discernment of God's inspiration was sound. For example, they were not threatened by the diverse emphases in the four Gospels of Matthew, Mark, Luke, and John. They recognized the same real Jesus revealed through these different books, and they bowed to the authority of these four. However, they saw a very different Jesus in other manuscripts.

Why did the church decide it needed an official canon? First, there were some clever teachers peddling books like *The Gospel of Thomas* to unsuspecting communities, and the church decided it needed a way of protecting people from fakes. Also,

Christians facing persecution and discrimination needed full confidence that they were risking their lives for something real. Even today, you may not have the time to learn the original languages, examine all the early documents for yourself, and discern which books sound authentic and which sound false. That's why it's helpful to know that other faithful people have done this important work. If you're interested in the detailed evidence for or against each ancient manuscript, a seminary library can point you to scholarly books on this subject.

Is my English translation accurate?

God inspired the biblical writers to pen their manuscripts. They wrote in Hebrew, Aramaic, and Greek on perishable materials. The original documents have long since crumbled. However, they were carefully copied by hand, and the copies were copied. Our modern Bibles are based on those copies.

Inspiration → Manuscripts → Copies → Translations

How accurate are the copies? Remarkably accurate. The scribes went to extraordinary lengths to double-check their work. The copies that have survived show minor variations on the level of the difference between "worked" and "has worked." Some names are spelled differently. *Old Testament copies show no variations that affect the meaning of the text.* When scholars compare Old Testament texts copied between 150 B.C. and 100 A.D. (the Dead Sea Scrolls) to a copy from 1006 A.D., they find "astounding similarity."[10] The various Greek copies of the New Testament are likewise nearly identical. There are variations that affect the meaning of a phrase, and some additions in late copies that don't exist in early ones, but *there are no variations that affect doctrine or the writer's basic point in a paragraph.*

In preparing English translations, scholars closely study all the variations in the Greek and Hebrew copies to choose the most reliable words whenever there is a discrepancy. Your Bible may include footnotes that let you know when there are textual variants. You can see for yourself that these variations don't affect the central ideas of the book.

How can I choose a good translation?

The Translation Spectrum[11]

"Formal Equivalency" or "Literal"	"Dynamic Equivalence"	"Free" or "Paraphrase"
NASB, RSV, NRSV	NIV, JB, GNB (TEV)	LB
KJB	NAB, NJB	PHILLIPS
NKJB	NEB	MESSAGE
MLB	REB	
	NLT	
Emphasizes original language's wording and word order	Emphasizes finding equivalent concepts in the translated language	Emphasizes simple and clear translation more than precision

Once the translators have settled on what they think is the best version of the original text, they have to render it into English. To do this, they have to decide how far they will go to bridge the historical gap between the ancient and modern language. In a literal translation like *The New American Standard Bible* (NASB), they try to stick as closely as possible to the exact words and grammar of the original language, while still making sense in English. A literal translation leaves the historical distance in grammar and language, allowing (or obliging) the reader to do as much interpretation as possible:

> *Wherefore it is necessary to be in subjection, not only because of wrath, but also for conscience' sake.* (Romans 13:5, NASB)

By contrast, a dynamic equivalence translation like *The New International Version* (NIV) "keeps historical distance on all historical and most factual matters, but 'updates' matters of language, grammar, and style."[12]

> *Therefore, it is necessary to submit to the authorities, not only because of possible punishment but also because of conscience.* (Romans 13:5, NIV)

You will generally find a dynamic equivalence version easier to read than a literal one. For close study, though, most people prefer a literal translation. You'll benefit even more if you compare several versions when you study. However, for daily reading, meditation, and memorization, it's a good idea to stick to one version that will become familiar to you.

Is a paraphrase useful?

A paraphrase is designed to narrow the historical gap as much as possible. Almost everything is updated so you can grasp meanings easily. While teams of scholars usually do literal and dynamic equivalence translations, one person usually writes a paraphrase. The quality of the paraphrase depends on that person's expertise in the meaning of the text and his or her gifts in writing English.

If you're just getting started in the Bible, a paraphrase can take you past many hurdles and into God's passion and brilliance. When you don't understand what the text is talking about, a paraphrase can give you one smart person's interpretation. And when you've read a passage in another version but want a fresh perspective, a paraphrase can help you see new things.

That's why you must live responsibly—not just to avoid punishment but also because it's the right way to live. (Romans 13:5, MSG)

A paraphrase shouldn't be your main version for study or memorization. However, you may find passages in a paraphrase so clearly and vividly expressed that you choose to meditate on and memorize those.

What if Bible teachers disagree about what a passage means?

The Bible is infallible. However, translators and teachers are not. Nor are you. The Holy Spirit has allowed portions of the church to stumble into error in the past, and He is likely to continue to allow this. This fact need not alarm you—human error has never yet defeated God's plan. God is able to bring you and the whole church to a safe destiny despite your mistakes.

Instead of worrying, let the inevitability of mistakes spur you to become spiritually mature so you can evaluate the Bible teaching you hear. Because you probably don't know all the areas in which God-honoring people disagree, seek input from a variety of sources and use your heart and brain to weigh the evidence. Choose teachers whose lives you respect and whose teaching is backed up by good Bible study methods. (For more on **sound Bible study methods,** see page 81.) Study the Bible on your own so you'll be equipped to assess what teachers say.

Also, familiarize yourself with the historical tradition of interpreting the Scriptures. Many mistaken interpretations have already surfaced in earlier centuries and been thoroughly debated. If you're not yet up to speed on the basics of the tradition, seek teachers who are and study books on the subject.

Beware of teachers who think they are never wrong. Beware of an attitude in yourself that needs to be right all the time: "God opposes the proud but gives grace to the humble" (James 4:6).

If you humbly seek God's guidance in choosing teachers and studying for yourself, you can trust Him to provide that guidance. He won't give you so much guidance that you will be infallible and never make mistakes, but He will keep you on a path of consistently growing in wisdom and learning from your mistakes. God *wants* to communicate with you. God *wants* to help you grow in humility and wisdom. Put your ultimate trust not in fallible humans but in the God who is active in your life and committed to your good.

What does it mean to say the Bible has authority?

Authority is the right to command, exact obedience, determine what is true, or judge. The Bible's authority means it has the right to:

- State what is true about God, humans, and the world
- Command what is right to do and forbid what is wrong
- Insist that people obey its commands as though they are from God
- Be the standard by which anyone can judge a truth or falsehood, or a right or wrong action.

> [Jesus] replied, "Blessed. . . are those who hear the word of God and obey it."
> (Luke 11:28)

The Bible derives its authority from God. As Creator and Sustainer of all that is, God has the right to say what is true about Himself and His creation, and what is right or wrong within it. According to the Bible, God does not declare these things arbitrarily—the truth and rightness flow from the essence of who God is. The Bible has authority because it is the written Word of God.

The Scriptures record many instances of God and Christ speaking and acting with authority. Often, the actions backed up the words. For example, Jesus demonstrated His authority over disease in order to prove His right to forgive sins (Matthew 9:1-8).

Likewise, God prefaced the Ten Commandments by pointing out, "I am the LORD your God, who brought you out of Egypt, out of the land of slavery." I, God, have demonstrated My authority over the forces of nature and over Pharaoh to the point where Pharaoh was forced to free you from slavery. Therefore, "You shall have no other gods before me" (Exodus 20:2-3). Freeing the people from slavery gave God the right to tell Israel what to do.

Most people who question the Bible's *accuracy* are really concerned to prove it has no *authority* in their lives.

Most people who question the Bible's *accuracy* are really concerned to prove it has no *authority* in their lives. If the Scriptures are telling the truth about God and Christ, then humans have no excuse to disobey them. And people are smart enough to see the costs involved in living by the commands and worldview of Scripture. "If I'm kind and honest, and everybody else in my workplace is committed to winning above all else, I'm going to look like a wimp and be left in the dust." Money, power, the approval of friends and colleagues—all are at stake when you choose to live according to the biblical worldview. The payoff—joy, peace, the approval of godly people, eternal intimacy with God—sometimes looks abstract and distant when you face the upfront costs of obedience.

This is why it's essential to immerse yourself both in the commands of Scripture and in the truths about God that prove His right to give you those commands. At the end of time, God will force all creation to bow to His authority. But God has delayed that day because He longs for your willing obedience and full-hearted love. Those cannot be forced. God and the Bible have authority over you whether you acknowledge them or not. But God's heart-cry is for you to recognize that He deserves that authority.

After all, it is personal experience that counts. And if anyone has reason to doubt the inspiration of the Bible, the certain yet simple test is to yield to its power, strive faithfully to follow its commands, act as it suggests. As a result, the conviction will irresistibly grow upon the mind seeking proof in this way, that its claim to be inspired of God is not to be questioned, but reverently received as just and undeniable.[13]

Is the truth out there?

All this talk of truth and falsehood, right and wrong, seems medieval to many people today. A philosophical position called deconstructionism says that all claims about truth are really masks for those who just want power. Deconstructionism has a point: *Many* claims about truth *are* motivated by power. In fact, people have been known to twist the words of the Bible in order to justify their cruelty toward other people. For instance, the Bible has been used to justify white supremacy.

However, taken as an absolute about all truth claims, deconstructionism goes too far. If there is a God who created the universe, then that God's perspective on life is the true one. That God's claims about truth are motivated not by power but simply by truth. Extreme deconstructionism says there is no Creator God. There are only interest groups competing for the power to say what goes.

The sister of deconstructionism is relativism. Relativism says there are no absolute truths. "Truth" is only what works in a given context. Truth depends completely on your point of view, and there is no God's-eye-view that is the standard by which all other perspectives are measured.

Deconstructionism and relativism treat reality like the laws of a democratic society. It would be as if the law of gravity were not written into the fabric of the universe. As if gravity were law only until an interest group could garner enough power to tip the balance on the Supreme Court or in Congress. As if gravity were law only as long as it made society run smoothly—but as soon as it seemed essential for humans to be weightless, citizens could vote and repeal gravity. Almost nobody actually believes such things about gravity, but many people believe them about ethical questions, the nature of God, and what happens when you die. These issues are supposedly decided by lobbying, voting, and personal preference.

Deconstructionism and relativism are worldview assumptions. If they are ingrained in your worldview, it may not be immediately obvious why they don't make sense of all parts of reality as you actually experience it. You may be editing your view of your experiences to fit these assumptions. The Bible invites you to question such assumptions. So if you're feeling queasy about the idea of "truth" and "right," suspend judgment for a while. Start reading a book of the Bible, looking for the reasons why the author believes God is the standard of (1) truth about reality and (2) right and wrong. See what you think.

What is Truth?

The Bible reflects the view that truth:
- Is a fitting relationship between a thought or statement and that which it is about
- Is not the same as belief or opinion
- Can be known
- Is simple

Take, for instance, your car's gas tank. A statement about your tank might be, "My gas tank contains gas." Truth would be a fitting relationship between that statement and the actual contents of your tank. This is not the same as a belief: "I believe my gas tank contains gas." Your belief will not affect the contents of your tank or the ability of your car to start. The truth about whether your tank is empty, however, would. If your belief corresponds to the actual contents of your tank, then your belief is true. Moreover, the truth about your tank can be known. Try to start the car. Dismantle the car and check. The truth or falsehood about your tank's contents is simple enough for a child to understand.

Some true beliefs are hard or currently impossible to verify. An example is, "Those who trust in Christ will be raised from death at the end of this age." However, the ability to verify it does not determine whether a statement is true.

Things can be true but not currently provable.

You believe many things not because you have personally verified them, but based on authority. Perhaps you are not a particle physicist, but you believe that all matter is composed of invisible particles called electrons, protons, and so on. That's fine. Reliable authority is a good source of true beliefs. However, because authorities are fallible, it is possible to have authority without truth. Sometimes authorities even lie. Your experience with authorities who lie may have led you to mistrust all authorities who make claims about truth. However, the dishonesty of some authorities does not mean it is foolish to believe anything on authority. [14]

Finally, you should know that the Bible presents ultimate truth not as a set of propositions but as a Person.

Jesus answered, "I am the way and the truth and the life." (John 14:6)

"I am the light of the world. Whoever follows me will never walk in darkness, but will have the light of life." (John 8:12)

According to the Bible, ultimate Truth and Reality is alive, personal, and eager to be known by you. The idea that anybody has authority to declare truth to you may feel scary. But He who is True is also committed to your good. He is no selfish dictator. And while many things are true or false, right or wrong, whether you like it or not, many other things truly are up to your personal preference.

> We do not know enough about the unknown to know that it is unknowable.
> —G. K. Chesterton[15]

The Transformed Life

We must allow the Word of God

to confront us, to disturb our security, to under-

mine our complacency and to overthrow our pat-

terns of thought and behavior.

John Stott[1]

How Can I Best Use the Bible to Grow Spiritually?

> For the word of God is living and active. Sharper than any double-edged sword, it penetrates even to dividing soul and spirit, joints and marrow; it judges the thoughts and attitudes of the heart.
>
> **Hebrews 4:12**

God created the world by speaking (Genesis 1:3,6,9,14,20,24). Every word God speaks has power to affect the universe. Because the Bible is the written utterance of God, His power works through it. Further, the Holy Spirit, whose job includes guiding you into all truth (John 16:13-15) and transforming you into the likeness of Christ (2 Corinthians 3:17-18), works through the Scripture to accomplish His tasks.

The Bible and salvation.

Salvation is the gracious act of God toward sinful, limited humans. The Bible speaks of God saving people from all sorts of evils, including enemies, disease, and slavery. However, the great theme of God's plan is God saving humans from slavery to sin and sin's consequences: the power of Satan (now) and death (ultimately). God saves you by the power of the Holy Spirit and through the death and resurrection of Christ. All you need to do to lay hold of this gracious gift is to put your faith in Christ as Savior and Lord.

So where does the Bible fit into this picture? First, the Bible is *the* source of definitive information about what salvation is and how you can be saved. The story of God saving Israel from slavery in Egypt forms the backdrop for understanding salvation. The Prophets look forward to the salvation of all God's people. The Gospels show Jesus doing His work as Savior. The letters explain salvation. Revelation depicts the final, complete salvation at the end of time. You don't need to understand salvation as well as a scholar in order to receive it, but you do need to understand it well enough to know what it's about and what's expected of you. What does it mean to have "saving faith" in Jesus Christ? The Bible will tell you. (For more on **God's plan,** see page 28.)

Another reason for reading what the Bible says about salvation is to spark gratitude.

Further, the Bible is not just a source of information about salvation; it is a powerful divine tool of salvation. God often does His works of power by speaking (Psalm 29:3-9; Isaiah 55:10-11). Multitudes of people have come to grips with God and put their faith in Christ as they read or heard the Scriptures.

Another reason for reading what the Bible says about salvation is to spark gratitude. If you have some vague idea that God has done something-or-other for you, you may be mildly grateful: "But he who has been forgiven little loves little" (Luke 7:47). If you wrap your mind around the hideous effects sin has had on your life, the horrible fate that would have awaited you had not God intervened through Christ, the lengths to which Christ went for your sake, and the joy that awaits you because of Christ— then you might be more inclined to love God with all your energy and passion.

Finally, understanding salvation helps you love your neighbor. You might have a friend who is mired in compulsive sin with a pile of mistaken notions about the Christian faith. The clearer your knowledge of the Bible, the more equipped you'll be to point your friend toward God.

A little understanding can change your life, and someone else's too.

From salvation to transformation.

The word *salvation* is usually used for the beginning stage of spiritual growth, although the Scriptures also say you "are being saved" (1 Corinthians 1:18) and that your full salvation awaits the kingdom's culmination (Romans 13:11). That ongoing process by which you "are being saved" includes what God is doing inside you and in the world around you. The part that's going on inside you is called *sanctification* (becoming holy as God is holy—1 Thessalonians 5:23) or *transformation* (taking on the worldview and values of Christ—Romans 8:29; 12:2; 2 Corinthians 3:18).

Just as salvation is by grace, so transformation is also by grace. "By grace" means:
- God takes the initiative to do it in you because of His love
- He does it in you by the power of the Holy Spirit
- There's nothing you can do to earn what God does in you

But while grace rules out earning, it doesn't rule out effort on your part. You need to cooperate with the Holy Spirit. You "work out" what God "works in" you. Philippians 2:12-13 says, "Continue to work out your salvation with fear and trembling, for it is God who works in you to will and to act according to his good purpose."

How does that happen? One way is through God's Word. The Bible is involved both in God's part and in your part of transformation. On one hand, the Word of God has divine power to affect your mind and heart. It is "the sword of the Spirit" (Ephesians 6:17). On the other hand, the Spirit is not going to pour the transforming truth of the Scriptures into your mind magically while you watch television. You need to put time and energy into taking it in.

Brain science and spiritual growth.

What Paul calls "the renewing of your mind" (Romans 12:2) is at least in part the renewing of your brain. Brain scientists divide learning into two categories: *explicit* and *implicit*.[2] Explicit learning is learning specific events and facts:

- What happened to you last Thursday
- The names of the twelve apostles
- The verse "In your anger do not sin" and its reference, Ephesians 4:26

You can often learn such things in one try, although memorizing twelve names or a verse and its reference can take some repetition. Still, this kind of thing is relatively easy to etch into your brain's cerebral cortex.

Implicit learning is quite different. It involves learning a procedure or skill:

- How to hit a golf ball
- How to act with love toward someone who has hurt you
- How to be angry but not sin

When you learn something implicitly, it feels like your body has learned it. Your body knows how to hit a golf ball. You know automatically how to feel anger but not sin. When you learn something implicitly, you often can't explain in words how it's done. You just know how to do it. It's hard to explain to somebody how to express love or how to feel anger but not sin.

Implicit learning is the way you form and change the way you see yourself and others. It happens *by practice*. It involves incremental shifting of connections between neurons in your brain. You may have to practice a golf swing thousands of times in order to lay down the neuronal pattern in your brain that makes the swing automatic. In the same way, you may have to practice something a thousand times before being angry without sinning becomes your reflex reaction to a situation.

Spiritual practice.

But what do you practice? Is it just a matter of facing a thousand annoying situations and doing your best? No. Because of sin, your best is incredibly weak in the beginning. On your own, you'll keep using your same old pattern (much like your old golf swing) over and over. Therefore, you might need to practice humbly opening yourself to the Holy Spirit's input several thousand times—both in stressful and non-stressful situations—before that part of the job becomes second nature. And there are other practices—solitude, community, silence, worship, Bible meditation, and so on—that also contribute to reprogramming your brain. These are like doing upper back exercises so your body is in shape to hit golf balls.

> The instruction "In your anger do not sin" is somewhat like the instruction "Run a twenty-mile marathon in less than four hours."

Some people think grace should mean you don't need spiritual practice. If you really have faith, these people reason, the Holy Spirit should just take over your brain and reprogram it so you can be angry without sin. If only that were true! But God doesn't want to control your brain. God wants you to be a mature person, not a robot. Find someone who's a real pro at love, and ask him how much time he's spent on the spiritual driving range practicing his swing. He may be embarrassed to tell you how much.

Studying the Bible involves a lot of explicit learning. You need to know information about how God sees the world. You need to know the fact that God has instructed His people to be angry but not sin. You need enough knowledge of the rest of the Bible to figure out what He means by being angry but not sinning. But ultimately, God has given you the Bible to help you with *implicit* learning. God wants you to acquire the ability to live according to His worldview.

The instruction "In your anger do not sin" is somewhat like the instruction "Run a twenty-mile marathon in less than four hours." If you're a couch potato, this instruction about marathon running is probably impossible for you to obey. You'll need to go into daily training for months or years, and this training will have to make major changes in your brain and body before you're able to obey this instruction. In the same way, you may not be capable today of being angry with someone but not sinning.

However, the Holy Spirit is eager to be your personal trainer. First of all, He can empower you to do things with your brain and body far beyond what you could ever do by practicing alone. On your own, you might be physically incapable of running twenty miles. On your own, you might be mentally incapable of feeling anger but responding without sin. The Spirit gives you the potential to be an Olympian with regard to loving God and others.

Second, the Spirit will guide you in using your Bible, life experiences, and other spiritual practices in an overall training process for feeling emotions without falling into sinful responses. When you read and think about what the Bible says about emotions, and when you read stories in the Bible about people feeling angry and either sinning or not sinning, you'll begin to get a good picture of what God means when He tells you to be angry but not sin. This new picture plays a part in retraining your brain. Meanwhile, if you spend time alone with God praying through biblical passages about emotions, time talking with other Christians about what you've learned, and time thinking about these insights as you go through your day, you'll further reshape the pattern in your brain. Then, when you encounter a situation that makes you angry, your brain won't be overwhelmed by the angry feelings. Instead, your anger will trigger that command you've internalized: "In your anger, don't sin." And this won't be just a powerless human thought, helpless in the face of your strong emotions—it will be the powerful Word of God free to work through your renewed mind. You will have given the Holy Spirit space and opportunity to use the Scripture to strengthen you in an important moment. The Spirit enables you to say *I can* and *I will* to God's command. That's transformation.

Right now, your brain is programmed to respond with anger to certain cues. But with help from the Holy Spirit, you can retrain your brain to associate the compassion of Jesus with those same cues. For example, if someone cuts you off on the highway, you might recall that when Jesus was on the cross, He forgave His persecutors. At first you may feel both anger at the other driver and shame that you aren't more like Jesus. But eventually, if you remember and apply how Jesus acted in a much more severe circumstance, the habit of forgiveness can become automatic. A good habit may take months or years to develop, and you will have to actively cooperate with the Holy Spirit, but the stories and teachings of the Bible can be an important part of retraining your habits.

Transformation vs. information.

In Jesus' day you did not administer a written test to find out if people understood the Sermon on the Mount. Instead, you watched how they lived. And you did not watch for mere external conformity to the wording of Jesus' teachings. You watched to see whether people adopted the attitude behind the instruction.

> "We must recognize, first of all, that the aim of the popular teacher in Jesus' time was not to impart information, but to make a significant change in the lives of the hearers. Of course that may require an information transfer, but it is a peculiarly modern notion that the aim of teaching is to bring people to know things that may have no effect at all on their lives."[3]

For example, Jesus told a parable about how the kingdom of heaven was like a treasure hidden in a field. When a man found it he went with joy and sold everything he had in order to buy the field (Matthew 13:44). The correct "application" of this Scripture is not to sigh and say, "Oh well, I guess I'm going to have to sacrifice a lot in order to be part of Jesus' kingdom." The correct application is not to make grudging sacrifices. The correct application is to see at the level of your gut how unbelievably valuable the kingdom is so that you *adopt the joy* of the man in the parable. Any sacrifices you make, any price you pay in serving Jesus in His kingdom wells up out of this joy. You can't manufacture this joy by sheer effort. You can't manufacture the gut belief that the kingdom is unbelievably valuable. If you don't believe it's that valuable, then you don't.

And if you don't, then the appropriate response to this Scripture is to begin a process of renewing your mind, of rewiring your brain and your heart. To do this, you meditate on the parable and let your experience struggle with it. Your conversation with God might go something like this:

The Scripture says I should think the kingdom of heaven is incredibly valuable. But deep down I don't think this. So:

- What is it that I'm not seeing about the kingdom?
- How is it that the kingdom ignited such joy in this treasure-finder?
- What would that joy look like and feel like?
- What are the things that I value so much that they seem more valuable than the kingdom?
- Why is there this gap between the joy the Scripture says I should have when I think about giving everything up to follow Jesus and the lack of joy I actually experience?
- Where do I see the seeds of joy in my heart already?
- Where do I see that I have already done some things that show that I do value the kingdom to some extent?
- Where are the seeds of the Spirit's work in my heart that I can build upon?
- God, I long for the joy of the treasure-finder. Please work in me to reveal Your kingdom in all its glory so I may value it and rejoice in giving up all to get it.

In Jesus' famous teaching about the tree and its fruit, the fruit is your behavior. The tree is your heart: your motives, attitudes, deepest beliefs, and emotions. Efforts at spiritual growth that focus on fruit—mechanical obedience to specific biblical instructions—will end in legalism. It's not possible to learn to love by that route. Instead, the aim of Bible study is to restore health to the tree—your heart—so that you produce good fruit "naturally," by your new nature. The Holy Spirit needs you to cooperate through your time and attention in order to get the teachings of the Bible deep into your heart where they will make a real difference in the tree.

> "No good tree bears bad fruit, nor does a bad tree bear good fruit. Each tree is recognized by its own fruit. People do not pick figs from thornbushes, or grapes from briers. The good man brings good things out of the good stored up in his heart, and the evil man brings evil things out of the evil stored up in his heart. For out of the overflow of his heart his mouth speaks."
> (Luke 6:43-45)

Beginning with your actual experience.

Allowing the Scripture to shine light on your experience—the things that are going on in your work, your health, your relationships—is a first step of transformation. Through these experiences, the Holy Spirit can go to work on your heart.

Experience→Scriptures→Struggle→Humility

"Experience is the matrix in which change is forged. Usually the realization that we have a need to change begins with an experience. . . . The experiences we are especially interested in here are those that are symptoms of deeper needs: things that reveal wrong attitudes, fears, destructive behaviors, and so on. . . .

"The appropriate response to an insight gained through experience is to turn to the Scriptures. . . . God's Word illuminates. It penetrates our clouds of self-deception and shows things as they really are. It takes courage to step into the light in this way. To be confronted with the truth about ourselves can be like getting caught with no clothes on. But we must see things as they are before we can do what needs to be done. . . .

"[To say *yes* to what the Scriptures say about us] takes a certain attitude on our part. It is humility. . . . Prayer and worship are the language of humility."[4]

Humility.

It takes courage to face what the Bible says about you. Then it takes humility to bend your knee to the God of the Bible who says both "you must learn to love" and "you cannot learn to love without cooperating with and depending on Me." It would be easier to swallow the Bible's teachings if you could just learn them and set out to do them. Or, it might be tolerable if you could say to God, "Fine. My heart is a mess and I can't love properly. So You do it. I'll go about my business the way I always have, and You zap me so I can love people. If You don't, it's not my fault." Unfortunately, neither of those options will get you anywhere. You're stuck with the constant, humbling dependence on your personal trainer, the Holy Spirit, who insists on retraining rather than zapping you.

Breadth: Reading the whole Bible.

Is it more helpful to read large portions of the Bible (even reading the whole thing each year or two)? Or is it more helpful to give extended time to small portions? There are good arguments for both approaches. One emphasizes breadth—getting the big picture. The other emphasizes depth—fully digesting what is read. The answer for you may be "Seek a balance of both" or "For this year, choose a method that fits the current needs in your growth process." The question to ask yourself is, *What method of systematic exposure to the Scriptures will best help me become captivated with God Himself and see the world as He sees it?*

The point of Bible reading is to know God and acquire God's worldview. (For more on **God** and **God's worldview,** see pages 22 and 115.) By reading the whole Bible, you can discover everything God has written about a given issue: trust or money or justice or sexuality. The Old Testament narratives contribute examples you

> "The approach that has helped me the most over the years has been to set aside time every day to read the Bible consecutively: something in the Old Testament, something in the New. A reading chart, which I keep in my Bible, helps me keep track of where I am. I pray as I read, asking God to give me understanding. When in the most unexpected places I come across something that addresses my situation, I stop to reflect. Clarity begins to replace my confusion. In the quiet I have heard God's instructions under the direction of the Holy Spirit. The learning experience may take a week; it may take six months or longer."[5]

can't get from the New Testament letters; the Law forms a background for under-standing the gospel. Reading the whole Bible shows you the big picture and all the available information. In this way, you won't base your view of God on a narrow slice of Scripture.

If you're reading large sections of Scripture, it's helpful to have one or two big questions in mind to focus your thinking. Otherwise, the words can just wash over you. You'll be amazed at how much you can learn if you read the whole Bible, or a whole section, looking for answers to one big question. (For **big picture questions,** see pages 28-39.)

Reading straight through from Genesis to Revelation may be hard for you if you're just beginning and have little background to make sense of the Old Testament. Use a study Bible that gives you Old Testament background, or start with the easier sections of Scripture and work up to the harder ones. (For a **plan to hit the highlights in a year,** see page 191.)

Depth: Meditating on a single passage.

There are equally good arguments in favor of spending more time on shorter sec-tions of Scripture. For example, a single exposure to a statement in the Bible may not renew your mind very much. You may need repeated exposures to internalize this truth, much as a person might hit two hundred golf balls to practice a single aspect of her swing. Repetition is what changes your brain. (For more on **brain sci-ence and spiritual growth,** see page 63.) Thus, if you spend two months fully digest-ing the meaning of Matthew 5, reflecting on it as you go through your day, and practicing it whenever the situation requires, you may see more lasting results than if you read all four Gospels during that time.

The goal of meditating on Scripture is to form the thoughts and habits of your mind so that it stays directed toward God. "When this is adequately done, a full heart of love will go out toward God, and joy and obedience will flood the life."[6]

Meditation on the Bible does not involve emptying your mind of thought. The Hebrew words for meditation mean "to muse about or consider deeply or at length" (Psalm 77:3; 119:15,23,48,78,148) or to "mutter or speak or read in an undertone"

(Joshua 1:8; Psalm 1:2; Isaiah 38:14).[8] In other words, there's a *thought* component and a *speech* component. To meditate on a passage of Scripture is to mutter or repeat it to yourself and to think deeply about it. Don't underestimate the value of reading a passage aloud or learning it well enough to say it aloud to yourself when you're driving or doing chores.

> ## Meditation
>
> • Restructures our thinking
> • Helps us learn God's thoughts and ways
> • Keeps us from "wandering"
> • Helps us fight temptation[7]

John 15:7-10 instructs you to abide in the Word of God. To abide is to live over a period of time in something. Meditation is how you abide in the Word. When you first read it, you briefly chew and swallow it. Then through thinking and muttering, you bring it up again into your thoughts and live in it over and over. You may muse over the same passage throughout the day. In this way it soaks deeply into your mind and heart. Abiding in God's Word leads naturally to abiding in His love and commandments.

Some people advocate doing study and meditation together. Others prefer to set aside a period of time for study and a separate time for meditation. Find an approach that works for you. (For more on **study,** see pages 81-91.)

Study and Meditation Together

1. Schedule a block of time.
2. Study a passage to understand what it means.
3. Take a walk away from noise, people, and hurry.
4. Talk to God about the passage. Ask Him what it means. How is this thought related to that thought? How can that be true in light of this? Ask God how He would like you to respond to it. Praise Him for what the passage reveals about Him. Confess your sin exposed by the passage. It's even okay to complain if the passage makes you uncomfortable! Just be honest and thoughtful.
5. Think in silence or mutter the passage back to yourself.[9]

Time and quiet.

In order to read, study, or meditate on the Scriptures effectively, you'll need to free yourself from busyness, noise, other people, and general distractions for some period of time each day, each week, or each month for what is often called quiet time. Some people advocate spending half an hour each day—or even fifteen minutes—in Bible reading and prayer. Others argue, "Better to have a two-hour block for study one day a week and then spend the next six days meditating on your insights than to have a superficial fifteen minutes seven days a week."[10] Whatever schedule you settle upon, let the function—digesting the Scriptures so they transform your thinking—determine the form.

You may need to reorganize other areas of your life in order to make time for the Bible. Busyness is considered a virtue in our culture, and contemplation is not, so you'll be swimming against the tide. However, there is really no other way to make progress in the spiritual life. You may need to struggle with God over your fears about what will happen to your career if you cut back your work time by two hours a week in order to spend time in the Scriptures and prayer. Or, two hours per week may mean giving up one video per week. If you have children, taking two hours per week alone to nourish your soul may seem selfish or impossible. However, your children will reap an enormous benefit: a parent whose soul is increasingly filled with the beauty of the kingdom of God.

Praying Through a Passage

The following is adapted from a method of prayer first published in France in 1688 by Madame Guyon:

1. Go to the Scriptures with a desire that God's revealed will shall be true for you.
2. Choose a passage with which you are already familiar, that doesn't require study at this point.

3. Read a small portion of the passage. Don't hurry. You can spend a month on the same passage if it's still nourishing you. In this method, you're aiming for depth, not quantity.

4. Treat the passage as a place in which you will have a holy meeting with God.

5. Ask the Holy Spirit to bring the realities expressed in the passage *fully* before your mind and into your life.

6. Observe what the passage says is true for the writer or the people being written about.

7. Allow yourself to yearn that the same might be true for you.

8. Ask, "What is my life like since this is true, and how shall I speak and act because of this?"

9. Affirm that this must be true.

10. Turn the passage into a prayer of praise or request. Ask God to make the passage true in your life.

11. Over time, as the Spirit works in you, come to the conviction that it *is* true.[11]

Step six assumes that you've taken the time to get an accurate interpretation or understanding of the passage. That's why you'll need to use a passage already familiar to you. You may have studied it before, or your pastor may have taught on it, or it may be something well-known, such as Psalm 23 or the Lord's Prayer. You'll be amazed at how much you can get out of a short and seemingly simple passage. (For more on **accurate interpretation,** see page 81.)

Don't push yourself on step eleven. You can't make yourself genuinely believe something down in your gut where it will affect your life. You can pretend to yourself that you believe it, but your actions will tell the real story. So give yourself time while doing what you *can* do. You can affirm the truth of the statement "Nothing can separate me from Christ's love." You can praise God for it. You can remind yourself of it as you go through this day and the next and the next. You can pray Romans 8:35 back to God. You can pour out to God your longing to know it's true. And you can allow the Holy Spirit time to work in your heart to settle the matter firmly. Trust Him, and He will do it.

If you've tried reading the Bible daily and have not seen much benefit, consider dedicating half a day to read through one of the Gospels. This may seem like a lot of time, but the idea is to completely immerse yourself in the world of Jesus. You need to give it enough time for the kingdom of God to become real to you. Imagine watching a great movie in fifteen-minute segments over the space of more than a week! Think how much more powerful the movie is, how much better it fills your mind with its world, if you watch it in one sitting.

People who love to play golf will easily dedicate three hours or more to a golf game. Some people are capable of watching four hours or more of television at one time, especially during an event like the Super Bowl. When you devote that kind of time to something, it fills your mind and affects how you think and what you do. If devoting half a day to entertainment a few times a year seems more "normal" than devoting half a day to the Scriptures, perhaps your heart believes that the Super Bowl nourishes you more than the

> ## Some Passages for Meditation
>
> • Exodus 20:1-20 (the Ten Commandments)
> • Psalm 23 (joy and peace available in the kingdom)
> • Matthew 5–7 (the Sermon on the Mount)
> • Matthew 6:9-15 (the Lord's Prayer)
> • Romans 8:28-39 (our security in Christ)
> • Philippians 2:1-18 (the attitude of Christ)
> • Philippians 4:1-9 (joy and peace)
> • Colossians 3:1-17 (how Christians live)
> • 1 John 1:5–2:2 (living in God's light)

Scriptures do. Maybe you can imagine being nourished and raised to a higher level of well-being by playing or watching a good game, but you can't imagine being nourished in that same way by the Bible. This is exactly the kind of heart belief that reading the Scriptures for an extended period of time alone in a quiet place is designed to overcome.

Treating questions with respect.

Whether you're studying a passage or praying through it, treat your questions with respect. If you don't understand something, or find it hard to believe something, or feel yourself pulling back from the God depicted in a passage, treat this confusion or negative feeling seriously. Listen for the voice of your heart saying, "This makes no sense to me." You may be able to clear up some of your questions by consulting a Bible dictionary. You can ask someone more mature in the faith. You can pray about your question. All of these are ways of treating your questions with respect. Remember, your heart is learning a new skill: be patient and gentle with your heart's questions and it will learn more quickly and thoroughly.

Sometimes your heart will ask questions as a defense against obedience. For example, perhaps you wonder about Joshua 6:17,21—why would a good God command Israel to kill not only all the humans in Jericho, but also all the livestock? Are you asking this question in order to convince yourself that the God of the Bible is cruel and may be safely ignored? Or is this question genuinely troubling you? Don't be distracted by defensive questions, but do take seriously your genuine questions. God will not be offended if you ask Him to help you make sense of His commands about Jericho. God wants you to understand about Jericho because He wants you to know why He deserves to be loved and worshiped. A good commentary will address questions like these. A good community, or even one friend who is mature in the faith, will also be invaluable.

How a community helps.

Transformation flourishes best in the context of a church or faith community. Nobody learns to love all by himself or herself. A vibrant faith community will:

- Help you understand what the Scripture means
- Help you struggle between what the Scripture says and the trials and temptations you experience
- Support you in choosing humility, obedience, and surrender to the Holy Spirit
- Offer you settings in which you can practice loving others
- Provide a place for the kind of corporate worship that makes God's magnificence more than just words on a page

Worship and Study

"Now we must not worship without study, for ignorant worship is of limited value and can be very dangerous. We may develop 'a zeal for God, but not according to knowledge' (Romans 10:2) and do great harm to ourselves and others. But worship must be added to study to complete the renewal of our mind through a willing absorption in the radiant person who is worthy of all praise. Study without worship is also dangerous, and the people of Jesus constantly suffer from its effects, especially in academic settings. To handle the things of God without worship is always to falsify them. In worship we are ascribing greatness, goodness, and glory to God. It is typical of worship that we put every possible aspect of our being into it, all of our sensuous, conceptual, active, and creative capacity. . . . Worship nevertheless imprints on our whole being the reality that we study. The effect is a radical disruption of the powers of evil in us and around us."[12]

Why Is Study Important?

The Sovereign LORD has given me an instructed tongue, to know the word that sustains the weary.

Isaiah 50:4

- How much do you want to know God?
- How much do you want to learn to love people well?
- If your answer is, "Not much," is that a problem?

Meditation and study are the two primary ways of taking in the truths of the Bible. They support each other. Study assures that you know what a passage means, and meditation gets that meaning from your head to your heart. Study without meditation can be lifeless. Meditation without study can reinforce your mistaken views.

Studying the Bible is reading closely, thinking about what you read, talking to people about it, and reading again. It's observing details like verbs as well as the big picture of what the writer is talking about in a whole book. Study means examining each paragraph. This doesn't have to be boring. It depends on how much you want to know what the text means!

For example, let's say your closest relationship is in danger of falling apart. Maybe it's your best friendship or your marriage. Someone gives you a book that contains what you need to know to save this relationship. Hopefully, you won't read this book casually, and you certainly won't just open it at random for inspiration. If you really want to save your relationship, and you really believe this book contains information that can help you do it, you'll probably pore over it. You might look at the table of contents to find the section that addresses the subject you most need to know about first. Then you might turn to that section and read it very carefully. You won't just take the author's ideas at random and run with them. You'll try to follow the logic of his argument. You'll look for his main points and how he illustrates them with stories. You'll look for the connection between a story and the main point. You'll have your own situation in mind, and you'll keep your eyes open for connections between your situation and the author's ideas, but hopefully you won't miss the author's point just because you're preoccupied with yourself.

> "The normal work of the Spirit is not to by-pass the Bible and pour information directly into our heads."[13]

This is study. It involves getting the author's main points and following the details. When you study a story in the history section of the Bible, you look for the main character and the main action, and then you follow the plot from point to point to point. When you study one of the New Testament letters, you follow the logic from paragraph to paragraph to paragraph. When you study the poetry of the Psalms, you picture the images the author is painting with words, you allow yourself to feel the feelings that the poetry raises, and you get the point just as you would get the point of a song.

Study can mean either boredom or revelation. It depends on how valuable you think the information is.

How Do I Figure Out
What a
Passage
Means?

Be good to your servant, GOD;
be as good as your Word.
Train me in good common sense;
I'm thoroughly committed
to living your way.
Before I learned to answer you,
I wandered all over the place,
but now I'm in step
with your Word.

Psalm 119:65-67, MSG

Perhaps, like many people, you've suspected that the Bible has been written in a secret code deliberately to keep its teachings mysterious. *Chaldeans. Atonement. Sanctification.* Is there a conspiracy to keep you in the dark?

No. "If you can talk and think, you can understand the Bible. . . . Bible study is basically just the application of common sense to the words of Scripture."[14] The principles of interpreting the Bible are just the same as the principles of interpreting anything you read or anything someone says to you.

Why is common sense important?

The Bible is written in ordinary human language, not in code or the language of an alien planet. Therefore, we can be confident that God intends us to interpret it according to the rules of ordinary language. God became a human being in order to reveal His divine nature to us in our world. In the same way, God speaks to us in a human form through human writers in a way that is "preserved perfect and uncontaminated while not being any less human."[15]

Hence, the challenge of interpreting poetry in the Bible is the challenge of interpreting poetry, not of interpreting some secret code. If you're not used to reading poetry, background information is available to help you. (For more on **what you can learn from the Psalms,** see page 151.) The same is true of biblical history or letters.

Some people treat the Bible like a Ouija board. They go to the Bible with a question, and they keep reading until they find a string of words that appears to answer their question. Should you homeschool your kids? "Depart, depart, go out from there! . . . Come out from it and be pure. . ." (Isaiah 52:11). This method is called *loose association.* It's unreliable because it's easy to find a sentence that seems to support your doing one thing or another. The only way to be sure you're not twisting the Bible to make it say something you want it to say is to stick with the meaning the author intended to give the sentence and the paragraph.

Another unreliable method is *Bible roulette.* Here, you open the Bible at random, and the passage upon which your eye falls is God's Word for you for today. "So Judas threw the money into the temple and left. Then he went away and hanged himself" (Matthew 27:5). If that were your verse for the day, what would God be telling you?

Loose association and Bible roulette are tempting but hazardous detours from the path of understanding what the Holy Spirit is saying in the Scriptures. The reliable route to understanding the Bible is the same as with anything else you read or hear: *your goal is to figure out what the author intended to say.*

What's the big deal with the "author's intent"?

One Meaning, Many Significances

When a speaker says something, there's only one interpretation of his words that correctly corresponds to the meaning he intended to convey. "In this sense a statement can only 'mean' one thing, no matter how many people read and interpret it. On the other hand, since every reader brings different experiences and knowledge to the text, the words of the author will have a slightly different impact on each reader. In this sense the meaning of the text will be different for every reader. I will refer to this subjective response of the reader as the *significance* of the text."[16]

The author's intent determines the meaning. Your unique situation and response affect the significance for you. But before you jump to the significance, it's essential to interpret correctly what the biblical author means to say. You'll need to discipline yourself to put the text first and yourself second. (For more on **you,** see page 38.)

The words of the Bible are not given simply to stimulate your own thinking. They're given to communicate things about God. The authors intended to communicate specific things through their stories and prophecies. The most important question to ask when you read the Bible is, "What is this author trying to tell me?" The question is not, "What goes through my mind when I read this?"

If you read the lyrics on a CD jacket, maybe it doesn't matter what the songwriter meant. But to say that the Bible has authority is to say that *the meanings the author intended to convey are the most important meanings.* God has authority. God speaks to the world through the Scriptures and says exactly what He wants to say. Humans don't get to come up with their own versions of what God is saying; they need to listen and hear what God is saying.

> Picture yourself reading a pamphlet describing tax regulations. Can you still be indifferent to the intent of the author and be satisfied with profound thoughts which occurred to you as you read? Of course not. When we want to know what another person means, then authorial intent becomes important. When the author has authority over us, we want to know what the author means. This is why authorial intent is particularly important in the interpretation of the Bible.[17]

How do I figure out the author's intent?

You do this in the same way you interpret anything you read or see on television. The rule of interpretation that you use every day is: *Think from the top down.* You automatically look at the following clues in this order:

- The type of communication
- The big idea of the largest unit of thought
- The big idea of the paragraph, stanza, or scene
- The sentence
- The word

The type of communication.

Imagine you're watching television. Somebody says, "The president's chief of staff is taking bribes." To make sense of this statement, the first step you take—automatically—is to verify what show you're watching. If it's a late night comedy show, then you interpret it according to the rules of TV comedy. You expect unsubstantiated gossip about political leaders to be amplified in order to produce humor. You know the real chief of staff is being discussed, but not entirely seriously. On the other hand, if you're watching a fictional drama about the White House, then you interpret the statement as a possible clue to the story. You immediately assume that "the president's chief of staff" is a fictional character, not the real person in Washington. Or again, if you're watching the evening news, then you expect this is a serious allegation about a real person. You expect evidence.

Comedy, drama, and news are three television *genres.* They are three types of communication, and you know the rules for interpreting each one. Similarly, history, prophecy, and letters are some of the genres in the Bible. The Psalms depend heavily on poetic imagery. When the Psalmist speaks of "God my Rock" (Psalm 42:9), you know he doesn't worship a literal rock. Paul's letters, on the other hand, depend largely on logic. Once you know the rules for interpreting poetry and letters, you'll be as skilled at this type of communication as you are with TV. (For more on **genres,** see pages 129-188.)

The big idea.

When you listen to someone talk, you don't interpret each sentence in isolation. You interpret sentences in the *context* of everything the person is saying. If you're really listening, you don't jump on one statement and tune out the rest. For if you tune out the big picture, you can easily misunderstand what's being said. (For an example of **reading a verse in context,** see pages 39-40.)

There are two levels of context or big ideas. First is the *largest unit of thought.* In one of the letters in the Bible, the largest unit of thought is the letter itself. So ask yourself, what is the letter about? If the letter is divided into sections, what is this section about? For example, Romans 12–15 is about how we should live in light of what God has done for us in Christ. In the Psalms, the largest unit of thought is the psalm. What is the whole psalm about? In the history books, what is the theme of the whole book? What is Genesis essentially about? What is the book of Judges about?

It takes some practice to learn to put words to what a whole book or psalm is about. But you're probably practiced at doing this with movies:

"What was the movie about?"

"Oh, it's a thriller [that's the genre, or type of communication] about a guy who's trying to prove he didn't really kill this person everybody thinks he killed [that's the big idea]."

If you haven't read the whole book, there are resources that can give you the big picture. (For more on **resources,** see page 105.)

The second level of context is the *paragraph* (in a letter) or *stanza* (of a poem like a psalm) or *scene* (in a narrative). You interpret the paragraph in light of what the whole letter is about. You interpret the scene in light of what the whole story is about. If you don't have time to read the whole letter or story, it's wise at least to read several paragraphs and get a sense of what the writer is saying. *Don't assume you know what a verse means if you don't know what the paragraph means. Don't assume you know what the paragraph means if you don't see how it relates to the paragraphs before and after.*

The Chapter and Verse Numbers Are Not Inspired

"Generally speaking, the basic unit of thought in the Bible is the paragraph. The chapter and verse notations were added in the sixteenth century by a Parisian publisher/printer named Robert Estienne (also known as Stephanus). . . . [W]e know that the Bible's chapters and verses are not necessarily the basic units of thought intended by their authors and should therefore be used primarily for Scripture reference and location, not necessarily as interpretive guides."[18]

Here are some clues to what the book, scene, or paragraph is about:[19]

- *Repetition.* Is a similar pattern repeated over and over in the story? For example, over and over in the book of Judges, Israel starts ignoring God, Israel gets overrun by oppressors, Israel cries out to God for help, and God sends a judge to rescue the people. That's a pattern. Is a word or phrase repeated? For example, "righteousness" turns up on numerous occasions in the book of Romans. "Love," "obey," and "believe" appear a lot in 1 John. In the books of Judges and Kings, look for the refrain, "[Name] did evil in the eyes of the Lord."

- *Key Words.* The key words that point to a big idea are often repeated. But sometime they aren't. "Shepherd" is a key word in Psalm 23.

- *Contrasts/Opposites.* Look for contrasted characters (the prophet vs. the wicked king) or ideas (sin vs. righteousness, death vs. life, light vs. darkness). Look for words like "but. . ." and "yet. . . ."

- *Comparisons/Similarities.* In Judges, notice the traits the judges have in common. In the Gospels, notice what the disciples have in common. In 1 John, notice how John compares love to obedience. Watch for the words "as. . ." and "like. . ."

- *Cause and Effect.* Sin produces death. God calls and people respond. God saves humans through Christ, and humans respond with love and obedience. David commits adultery and the ripples spread through his family and his kingdom. Look for words like "if. . . then," "therefore. . . ," and "then. . . ."
- *Train of Thought.* How is this paragraph connected to the previous one? How does this scene build on the one before?

The sentence.

Interpret a sentence in light of what the whole paragraph or scene is about. Think *context:* Each sentence develops the big idea of the paragraph. Think *grammar:* The subject and verb are the focus of a sentence. The subject is the person or thing doing the action. The verb is the action.

Sentence: Jesus wept.
Subject: Jesus
Verb: wept

Is the verb in the past, present, or future? Is it a one-time event ("we were saved") or ongoing ("we are being saved")? Are there connecting words like "but" or "and" that point to contrast or train of thought?

If grammar gives you nightmarish flashbacks to seventh grade, talk to God about it. Close reading takes more work for some people than for others. Keep your goal in mind: These are the actual words of the Eternal God who wants you to understand who He is and how life works.

Pronouns (we, you, us, them) trip up many people. When Paul says, "We are therefore Christ's ambassadors" (2 Corinthians 5:20), does "we" refer to all Christians, all the apostles, or Paul's mission team? In 2 Corinthians 1–5, he uses "we" a lot, and if you read the whole *context*, you can figure out who "we" are in each case.

The word.

Sometimes the meaning of a paragraph hinges on the meaning of a word. For example, in Romans 8, Paul repeatedly uses the Greek word *sarx*, which is literally "the flesh" (NASB, NKJV, NRSV) and may mean "the sinful nature" (NIV, NLT), "the lower nature" (NEB), or "the self" (NJB). Another important word in Romans is "righteousness." A Bible dictionary can help you understand the range of meanings a word can have. It's a good idea to look up key words like "flesh" and "righteousness" in a Bible dictionary so that you have more than a vague idea of what the word means.

Look up key verbs as well. Did you know that "save" and "heal" are the same word in Greek? A Bible dictionary can give you that information.

In addition to a Bible dictionary, two other resources for understanding individual words are a concordance and an English dictionary. (For more on **resources,** see page 105.)

Wise Word Studies

Because we can learn so much from word studies, it's tempting to push them too far. Here are three rules to follow:

First, usage determines meaning. It's interesting to know that the word awful comes from the root word awe. But if you know what awe means, you don't necessarily understand what awful means. The root gives you some clues, but it's more important to know how this word was used at the time the writer wrote.

Second, the more data you have, the more reliable your conclusion is. If the word appears only once in the Bible and nowhere else in any ancient Greek writings that still exist, then scholars don't have a lot of data about all the possible meanings the word could have. What if one surfer magazine contained the only instance of the word awesome that a future scholar had to work with? Would that scholar figure out what it means to say in English that God is awesome?

The context of the whole paragraph is often the best guide to what the word means. Word studies are not a magic solution to interpreting all passages. It's helpful to do word study research, but you can get a long way if you use a good Bible translation, read carefully from paragraph to paragraph to paragraph, and follow the reasoning or the story.[20]

Jesus called Himself "humble in heart" (Matthew 11:29). You can learn a lot from looking up "humble" in a dictionary, but you can learn even more from reading the rest of Matthew. What did humility look like in Jesus' case? Surely it can't mean thinking poorly of oneself—Jesus went around acting like God! Even if you just read Matthew 11:25-30, this context can help you understand what "humble" meant to Jesus.

You can see that studying the Bible involves a range of skills from analyzing the details to comprehending the big picture. Over time, you can develop any of these skills. Still, most people are more gifted at some dimensions of study than others. One benefit of Christian community is that it gathers people with diverse gifts to tackle the essential tasks of spiritual growth. Consider meeting with a group to study a book of the Bible. You'll find that one person is good at putting the big ideas into words that all can understand. Another will catch on quickly to comparisons, contrasts, and train of thought. A third will enjoy investing time in individual words and reporting her findings to the group. So team up! You were never meant to tackle the Christian life alone.

Won't the Holy Spirit tell me whatever He wants through the Bible?

Some people question whether "what the author intended to say" is what matters. They argue that the Holy Spirit will guide any real Christian to learn just what He wants that person to learn when the person reads any passage in the Scripture.

Because the Bible is the divine Word of God, doesn't it limit God's power if we read it like any other book? Can't we just read it however we choose and trust that God will transform us according to His supernatural power?[21]

What the Spirit Will Do

• Help you as you do your best to discern the meaning of the text
• Show you the significance of the text for your life
• Enliven the words of Scripture so that they penetrate not just your head but also your heart

Among those who support this view, some think that it's okay to look for historical background or the context of a verse when you're *studying* the Bible, but you don't have to do that when reading the Bible for *devotional* purposes. The idea here is that when you're reading the Bible *spiritually*, you expect the Holy Spirit to talk to you through one sentence or another of the text, and it doesn't matter what the text originally meant.

Those who say this usually don't realize that their view dishonors the Holy Spirit. But think about it. The Holy Spirit went to the trouble to choose specific persons in specific times and places to write specific kinds of writings. He said what He meant to say to the Corinthians. He doesn't want His words twisted to mean something He didn't intend to say.

That's why the original meaning the Spirit intended to convey to the Corinthians is the only *meaning* of 1 Corinthians. If you're committed to sticking to the one meaning of the text, the Spirit will guide you in seeing the unique *significance* this text has for you. This significance will never contradict the text's meaning, so part of listening to the Spirit is paying attention to the meaning He put into the text from the beginning.

What the Spirit Will Not Do

• Do your homework for you
• Override your determination to see in the Bible what you want to see

Context is Crucial

"As an author, I cringe to think what would happen if people read my books in the same way they read the Bible. What if a reader picked up one of my books and arbitrarily turned to a stray sentence or paragraph on page 127? Probably it would not make sense; possibly the passage, wrenched out of its context, might convey the opposite of what I intended to communicate."[22]

—Philip Yancey

What's the Biggest Barrier to Understanding a Bible Passage?

We sometimes tend to think we know all we need to know. . . but sometimes our humble hearts can help us more than our proud minds.

1 Corinthians 8:2 MSG

"Communication works, when it does work, because the author is counting on the pre-understanding of the reader."[23] For example, you ask your friend, "How was the movie?" He replies, "It was cool." Is this a statement about the air conditioning in the theater? Probably not. How do you know? You're familiar with the slang, metaphorical use of the word "cool." You have a *pre-understanding* of early twenty-first-century American English.

But imagine someone from a non-English-speaking country who has learned English by studying the works of Jane Austen. This person would try to make sense of your friend's statement in the context of the ways in which Austen used "cool" in nineteenth-century England. There would be an understanding gap. When there's a gap between the pre-understanding the speaker expects and the pre-understanding the hearer has, communication breaks down.

The biblical writers wrote in the familiar language of their own place and time. Paul assumed his readers:

- Knew Greek as it was used by the common people in the first century A.D.
- Knew the customs of the Roman Empire
- Knew the basic geography of the Roman Empire
- Knew a fair amount of Old Testament stories and teaching

- Remembered everything he had said to them when he visited their town
- Remembered things that had happened when he visited their town

You don't bring this pre-understanding to the table. You have a language gap, a cultural gap, a geography gap, and an experiential gap. Your pre-understanding gap is often your biggest barrier to interpreting a biblical text. Fortunately, there is now a wide menu of resources to help you bridge that gap.

However, you can't bridge a gap you don't know you have. If you come from a denominational tradition that gives you a set of lenses through which to read the Bible, you may think you already know what a passage is supposed to mean before you read it. Even if you have no church background, you bring your pre-understood ideas about God, sin, truth, human nature, and many other subjects whenever you open the Scriptures. Abandoning your pre-understanding is not an option. Instead, your goal is to correct it. You're aiming to close the gap between the knowledge you actually bring to the text and the knowledge you need to bring.

Here are five steps to closing the gap:[24]

Be willing to change your mind.

If you can't stand to be wrong, you'll have trouble admitting that your initial interpretation of a passage might need correction.

"As Christians we are called to believe the truth and defend it passionately. There is a great difference, however, between believing 'The Bible is infallibly true' and 'My understanding of the Bible is infallibly true.'"[25]

Gather new information.

Use a dictionary to be sure you understand the key words in a passage. Use a commentary for essential information about context, grammar, or historical background. (For more on **resources,** see page 105.)

Follow the author's lead.

Don't pull verses out of context in order to prove a point you want to make. Be sure you understand the paragraph in which the verse occurs and the point the author wanted to make. Consider Luke 12:33, in which Jesus commands, "Sell your possessions and give to the poor." This is a fairly straightforward instruction, isn't it? Not much interpreting to do here. What if someone used that verse to convince you that God wants you to immediately sell everything you own, give all the money away, and become a street preacher? Well, before you either go sell your clothes or completely dismiss this verse as not applying to you literally, you may want to read Luke 12 in its entirety. (For more on the **author's intent,** see page 82.)

Imagine all the possibilities.

You don't have to throw out your current interpretation immediately. But do a thought experiment. Suppose you're wrong about Luke 12:33. Suppose Jesus intends all Christians in all times and places to follow this command to the letter. What would that mean? How would that affect your understanding of Luke 12 as a whole? How would it affect your understanding of the gospel, of what it means to be a Christian? What other beliefs about life would you have to change?

Seek consistency.

Christians believe the Bible speaks the truth. Ultimately, "the truth is always consistent with other truth. If the Bible is true in what it says, then its message is consistent within itself and consistent with the real world. We cannot rest, therefore, with an interpretation that is inconsistent with the rest of the Bible or with reality. We are always seeking a coherent understanding of the Bible and of life."[26]

So, for example, one scriptural passage seems to say that humans get to choose freely whether they will or won't put their faith in Christ. Another passage seems to say that God chooses everyone who will have faith. Somehow, your interpretations of these two passages must be consistent with each other and with reality. You don't get to throw out one passage and keep the other. You don't bend and twist one until you can make it fit the other; psychological gymnastics is not the goal. Instead, you may have to live with some tension between passages, some mystery and paradox, some struggle. But ultimately you know that these two passages fit into a large, true understanding of how God actually works. Wise Bible students have studied these very passages, and you can read the results of their reflections in commentaries and other books. You can even draw your own conclusions and add them to the church's ongoing conversation on this subject.

Committed to Consistency

"If my interpretation of a passage comes into conflict with my pre-understanding of the rest of the Bible, which one do I change? My pre-understanding about the real world is equally subject to error. If my conclusions from the Bible contradict my pre-understanding about life and reality, which do I reject?. . .

"The search for consistency is absolutely necessary. If we cannot reconcile our interpretation of a passage with our understanding of the rest of the Bible, or with our worldview, then *something is wrong*. Yet too many Christians have allowed themselves to amass an incoherent and conflicting set of beliefs about life and the Bible. . . . It is not always easy to know just where we have gone wrong, but knowing *that* we have gone wrong is an important step in itself."[27]

Some people think they don't interpret the Bible; they just read it. To them, the meaning is obvious. But the meaning is obvious only if you bring the right assumptions to the text. And your assumptions can easily be wrong. For example, tell a five-year-old, "Go put on some clean socks." This instruction seems straightforward. But don't be surprised if the child comes back wearing clean socks over his dirty ones. Just as it takes time for a child to adopt all the right assumptions about clothes so she can understand her mother's meaning, so it will take you time to learn the assumptions you need to understand the Scriptures.

What Background Information Can Help Me Understand a Bible Passage?

It is not good to have zeal without knowledge, nor to be hasty and miss the way.

Proverbs 19:2

Background information about the biblical world and biblical languages helps to close the understanding gap between you and the writers of the Scripture.

Humility

"My problem is not so much that I do not live in the first century, but that I do live in the twenty-first. My head is overflowing with facts, beliefs, ideas, and experiences, many of which will mislead me if I read them into the Bible. For this reason, the first step toward interpretive skill is not to buy a Bible encyclopedia, but to change our way of thinking. We need to become sensitive to the potential differences between my world and the biblical world. The text is not going to flash a sign at me: *Insert Missing Background Info Here.* I have to be prepared to exercise my imagination. Most importantly I need to bring a certain intellectual humility. The background understanding I bring to the text may be the wrong one, and I need to be prepared, even eager, to acknowledge that and correct it. Understanding requires humility; this is true in Bible study as well as anything else."[28]

Useful background information includes:

- **Language:** Something is always lost in translating from one language to another. In a famous case, the words of Jesus, "The Spirit is willing but the flesh is weak," were translated from English to Russian and back again. The result was, "The liquor is good but the meat is bad." Translating is even harder from an ancient to a modern language. To bridge the language gap, consider obtaining at least a couple of good English translations and a Bible dictionary. (For more on **word studies,** see page 88. For more on **translations** and **Bible dictionaries,** see page 105.)
- **Culture:** How important was family honor at that time?
- **History:** Who were the Assyrians?
- **Geography:** How big is the Sea of Galilee?

Culture.

Some details about ancient culture are simply interesting and help you picture biblical events vividly. For example, Luke 7:36 says Jesus "reclined at the table." This may sound odd until you know that it was customary in ancient times to dine while lying on one's left side on a couch or mat, leaning on one's left arm, and eating with one's right hand. If you can picture this, you can see how the woman who anointed Jesus' feet at a dinner party was able to reach them (Luke 7:36-50). They weren't hidden under a table; they were stretched out away from the table. They were also bare (people removed their sandals indoors).

Some cultural details enable you to understand how people in a story may have felt. Luke 7:38 says the woman wiped Jesus' feet with her hair. In that culture, a woman's hair was a strong symbol of her sexuality. Proper women kept their hair tied up in public. It was considered scandalous for a woman to let down her hair with anyone but her most intimate family. This woman not only untied her hair but actually touched it to the bare feet of a man she didn't know! This was the ancient equivalent of disrobing in public and acting provocatively toward a stranger. If you know this, you can imagine how the other guests at the dinner party felt about the woman for doing this and about Jesus for letting her.

The most important cultural details let you know what people valued in ancient times. Then you can understand when Jesus or someone else was challenging the values—the worldview—of His time. You can also reflect on how the values of your culture stack up against the values of Jesus or His culture. For example, ancient people intensely valued honor and shame. To "have honor" meant to have your worth as a person publicly acknowledged. To "have shame" meant to be concerned about your honor. To "be shamed" meant to lose your honor, to be viewed as worthless. Your honor was wrapped up in the honor of your group—your family, your ethnic group, your town. If you were shamed, your whole family was shamed (and they let you know about it). Honor was so essential to your feeling of being okay that you'd rather lose all your money and your right arm than have the people around you see you as a loser.

If you can feel your way into this value system, then you'll get the full impact of Luke 7:36-50. This woman publicly humiliated herself. She trashed every shred of honor she had left in order to express love for Jesus. Jesus Himself placed His honor on the line by letting this "woman who had lived a sinful life" (read: loser) throw herself at Him. In order to protect His honor, He should have rejected anyone who acted shamefully. Instead, He honored her. He said her shameful act of kissing His feet was actually an honorable act. Even more, He claimed the right to define the standards of honor, to declare who deserved honor and who didn't. Jesus valued honor, but He rewrote the rules of honor.

If you're not used to thinking about values, this discussion of honor may seem lofty. But one of the main things the Holy Spirit wants to do with the Bible in your life is to *realign your values to those of God*. So you can ask yourself:

- How important is honor in my world?
- What wins honor in my world? (For example, income.)

Values Questions

- What did people at that time value?
- What do the people in this story value?
- What does Jesus or God value in this story?
- In this letter, what does Paul value?
- According to this prophet, what does God value?
- How does Jesus or God challenge the values of that culture?
- What does my culture value?
- How do my culture's values stack up against God's?
- To what extent do my actions reflect my culture's values rather than God's?

- What wins honor in Jesus' eyes?
- Am I willing to sacrifice my reputation in my culture in order to have honor in Jesus' eyes?

History.

The point of learning biblical history is not to win trivia games. It doesn't matter if you can recite the names of the kings or judges from memory. What you really need is a working knowledge of the main events and the order in which they occurred.

For example, in the New Testament the Roman army is occupying the Holy Land. There's a lot of talk about paying taxes to Caesar (the Roman emperor) and about Roman soldiers doing this and that. The occupation colors what the Jews expect from their promised Messiah or king. The New Testament will make more sense if you learn basic answers to questions like: What's the history of the Holy Land and the Jewish nation? How did Rome end up in charge? How did Roman rule affect Jesus' life and death, Paul's ministry, and the growth of the church?

Jesus is called "son of David." Who was David? Under what circumstances did he become king in Israel? How did his descendants lose the throne? The people who called Jesus "son of David" knew all that information, and if you know it too, you can understand the full impact of their giving Him that title.

This is not information for the sake of information. It's information in the service of responding to the biblical text in the way the Holy Spirit intends. You can get a long way with a basic book on biblical history. (For more on **what you can learn from history,** see page 129.)

Basic Bible History

- God creates the world (Genesis 1–2)
- Humans fall into sin (Genesis 3)
- God protects a remnant from the great flood (Genesis 6–9)
- God calls Abraham and his family (Genesis 12–36)
- The family moves to Egypt under Joseph's protection (Genesis 37–50)
- Egyptians enslave Israelites; Moses leads the slaves to freedom (Exodus)
- Israelites struggle to occupy the Promised Land (Joshua, Judges)
- God allows Israel to have human kings (1 & 2 Samuel)
- The kingdom of David and Solomon splits after Solomon's death (931 B.C., 1 Kings 11–12)
- The two kingdoms (Israel and Judah) slide downhill morally (1 & 2 Kings, Prophets)
- God lets Assyria destroy Israel (722 B.C., 2 Kings 17)
- God lets Babylon destroy Judah and carry the Jews into exile (605–535 B.C., 2 Kings 24–25, Jeremiah)
- God prompts Persians to let Jews return and rebuild Jerusalem (535–440 B.C., Ezra, Nehemiah)
- Judah struggles with internal strife and external oppression from Persian, Greek, and Roman empires (535 B.C. –70 A.D.)
- Jesus born (about 4 B.C.)
- Jesus crucified (about 33 A.D.)
- Followers of Jesus spread the gospel to urban centers of the Roman Empire (33–62 A.D.)

Geography.

Place names frustrate many readers of Scripture. They're often hard to pronounce, you don't know which ones are important to remember, and you have no idea where they are. Still, you'll be surprised at how much clearer the text will be if you know a little geography.

For example, consider the tiny piece of real estate called the Holy Land, the Promised Land, Canaan, Israel, Judah/Judea, Galilee, Samaria, or Palestine. Most of the action in the Bible takes place there. God promised this land to the family of Abraham, and for the next several thousand

> ## The Three Rules of Real Estate:
>
> Location
> Location
> Location

years, a drama unfolded there. Of course, God could have gone into business with a family in the southern tip of South America. In that out-of-the-way spot, this family would have been left alone for centuries and could have become a great nation in peace. But God deliberately chose a place whose geography guaranteed constant upheaval.

The Holy Land is a bridge between Africa and Asia. Egypt (in north Africa) had a longstanding civilization built around a fertile river, the Nile. The region now called Iran and Iraq also developed strong but volatile civilizations built around two other fertile rivers, the Tigris and the Euphrates. In order to get from Iran-Iraq to Egypt, traders and armies had to pass through the Holy Land. The Holy Land has no river that provides its water, so the inhabitants have to depend on rainfall.

God owns the whole planet, but He focused His plan on a region that would be constantly vulnerable, fought over by empire after empire. Cultures would constantly mix there, as traders and soldiers brought their ideas and practices with them. It's no accident that the Middle East has been a hot spot throughout recorded history. Geography assures it.

Until you get into the mind-set of the Old Testament, it's hard to imagine how big a role land played both in people's minds and in God's plan. The land was an essential part of the covenant (agreement) between God and Israel. When God allowed invaders to wrest the land from the Jews and send them into exile, it was a calamity. When God allowed a remnant to return and rebuild the nation, it was a miracle. If you wonder whether geography matters, talk to an Israeli or a Palestinian today.

Likewise, geography was key to the spread of the gospel. Paul didn't wander randomly from place to place; he chose strategic cities throughout the Roman Empire. Because he couldn't go everywhere personally, he set up base camps in Thessalonica,

Philippi, Corinth, Ephesus, Rome, and elsewhere from which other people could spread the gospel into their regions.

Even individual stories will make more sense if you know geography. When you read about the disciples going out on the Sea of Galilee in a storm, it's helpful to know the Sea of Galilee is about twelve miles long and four miles wide, with mountains around it that whip up fierce winds. This is a big lake with sudden nasty weather.

God owns the whole planet, but He focused His plan on a region that would be constantly vulnerable, fought over by empire after empire.

Distances matter. Abraham traveled by camel from Babylonia (Iraq) to Canaan (Palestine). How far is that, and how long would the trip have taken? Jesus walked from Jerusalem to Galilee through Samaria. How far is that? Paul walked across Turkey. That's an incredible journey on foot.

So when you hit a place name in the Scriptures, pause to look it up on the map in the back of your Bible, a Bible atlas, or a Bible dictionary. Where is it? How far is it from somewhere else named in this text? What's important about it? How does its geography affect the biblical events? Usually a map (for visual information) plus a dictionary or encyclopedia entry can tell you all you need to know. Also, more and more of this information is available on the Internet.

Where Do I Find Useful
Background
Information?

Here are some resources that can give you the background you need. Depending on how serious you are about study, you probably don't need to own all of them. A couple of good translations, an English dictionary, a Bible dictionary, a concordance, and a few maps may carry you for a long time.

A good translation.

Unless you're prepared to learn Hebrew and Greek, your best tool for understanding words and grammar in the Bible is a good translation. Well-trained people have put enormous effort into selecting the English words in good translations. Your next language tool will be a *second* translation. Then you can compare what two different teams of translators think the words and sentences mean. (For more on **translations,** see page 49.)

An English dictionary.

Let's say, for example, a passage uses the word *exhort*. You might look up that word to see exactly what it means in English. An English dictionary is good for words that don't have a distinct usage in the Bible, words that are essentially "secular." That's because an English dictionary is designed around everyday English usage.

A Bible dictionary.

On the other hand, perhaps you want to know what *righteousness* means. This word has a distinct history of meaning from the earliest books of the Old Testament, through the later ones, into the words of Jesus, and finally in the New Testament letters. It means something in Jewish and Christian usage that the secular writers of English dictionaries don't always consider. For a word like this, a Bible dictionary is more useful.

While an English dictionary might tell you *righteousness* means "meeting the standard of what is right and just,"[29] a Bible dictionary will stress that it signifies "right relationship" with God and others.[30] The English dictionary isn't wrong about English usage, but it doesn't reflect biblical usage. In the Bible, righteousness is more about right relationship than about keeping rules. If you think "rules" instead of "relationship" whenever you see *righteous* in the Bible, you'll put the wrong spin on those passages.

A concordance.

This is an alphabetical index of key words used in the Bible along with the verse references throughout the Bible where those words can be found. Usually, you'll find the verse reference and part of the sentence that includes the word.

> **besiege**
> he shall **b.** you in gates. *Deut* 28:52
> if enemies **b.** you. *1 Ki* 8:37

You may have a condensed concordance in the back of your Bible that offers a handful of major verses for each major word. However, an *exhaustive* concordance is more useful for study. An exhaustive concordance includes all the references for all the words. Most publishers of major Bible translations publish an exhaustive concordance for that translation. (A concordance lists the references for each *English* word, so it's tied to a single translation.)

A good concordance will have a Greek and Hebrew section in the back. There you'll find the Greek or Hebrew word and its various meanings. Beside each entry in the main (English) section, you'll find a number that will point you to the right Greek or Hebrew word in the back. This system will show you that there are several different Greek words that may be translated as "sick" in English, and each one has a slightly different flavor. Conversely, behind "saved" and "healed" lies a single Greek word.

A Bible atlas.

This will show you maps of the Middle East with the place names as they were in the time of Abraham or David or Jesus. It will show possible routes by which Moses led the Israelites out of Egypt, how Canaan looked when Joshua was invading it, and where Paul went on each of his mission trips. A good one will tell you why various geographical features are important.

A computer Bible.

If you enjoy working on computer, most major Bible translations are available on CD-ROM. The built-in search function works like an exhaustive concordance. Bible dictionaries, encyclopedias, and atlases are also available for computers.

A study Bible.

Most of these include cross-references from one verse to other verses that relate in some way. Cross-references are not inspired and so are only as good as the authors of the study Bible. The same is true for the notes about the text's meaning, the cultural background, or the application for today.

A Bible encyclopedia.

This is usually a multi-volume work that goes into more depth than a Bible dictionary. It includes the authors' assessment of archaeological evidence and other historical sources.

A history survey.

A book that overviews Old Testament or New Testament history can tell you everything you need and more about ancient times.

Commentaries.

For each book of the Bible, scholars have written commentaries from an immense variety of points of view. Some commentaries are highly academic; others are for lay-people who want to apply the text to their lives. For your purposes, a useful commentary will give you the kind of cultural, historical, and geographic background that will enable you to understand what the text would have meant to its first readers.

Books and tapes by Bible teachers.

These aren't usually listed as Bible study tools, but more and more laypeople are relying on them. They normally include explanation of what a passage means, some relevant information about culture or language, vivid storytelling, and application to modern life. Use these cautiously.

Of all these tools, the concordance is the least dependent upon a modern author's viewpoint. A translation grows from hundreds of interpretive judgments by a team of scholars. A Bible dictionary also reflects the theological outlook of its writers. A study Bible or Bible encyclopedia has even more of the authors' interpretations. A commentary is intentionally one scholar's attempt to pull together all of the knowledge that scholar has about that biblical text. A Bible teacher's book is obviously his or her take on the Scripture and its significance today. It's not bad to consult any of these as long as you don't trust them uncritically. They are only as good as the scholar or Bible teacher who produces them. Sometimes legends about Bible times ("In those days, the Camel's Gate was a small door in the wall of Jerusalem. . . ") get handed down from commentator to teacher. Far too often, the commentator's bias gets in the way of what Jesus or Paul wanted to say. *The Bible is inerrant, but teachers and commentators are not.* So, when you go to such sources for background:

- Treat them as human, and don't be afraid to ask, "Who says so?"
- Don't spend so much time reading secondary sources that you aren't immersed in the Scriptures themselves.
- Learn as much as you can about the biblical world, but cautiously. Take care that the facts you read or hear are really facts.

• Subject any background facts to the ruthless scrutiny of the context of the particular passage.

For example, you're reading 1 Corinthians 11 about women's headcoverings. Your study Bible tells you what the custom was among Jewish women in Paul's day. You might ask questions like, "How do the writers of my study Bible know this? Can I verify this from a Bible encyclopedia or commentary? Is it relevant—does the context of this passage have anything to do with Jewish customs? Does the situation in Corinth have to do with Jewish women or Greek women?"

The point is to be neither naïve nor cynical about sources of background information. If you choose them well, they can help bring the text alive for you.

What Does It Mean to
Take the
Bible Literally?

"The word 'literal' has two different meanings. . . . Literal can mean 'non-figurative,' or 'as the author intended.'"[31] To interpret the Bible non-figuratively is to believe that Jesus meant you to picture a literal loaf of flat wheat bread when He said, "I am the bread of life." That makes no sense. *The correct way to take the Bible literally is to interpret each statement as the author intended.* That means interpreting it according to the normal language conventions at the time the book was written. You assume that words and phrases mean what they meant at that time. Figurative language is a natural aspect of language, so you'll interpret figurative language figuratively. When you read, "the LORD is my shepherd," you won't assume the psalm was written by a sheep. You'll assume it was written by someone who was speaking figuratively of himself as being like a sheep.

"The LORD is my shepherd" is a metaphor. A metaphor is a figure of speech that uses an object or an idea to suggest a similarity. X is like Y in certain ways. Normally, the speaker is not saying X is like Y in every imaginable way. For example, if you say, "Joe is on fire for Jesus," fire is a metaphor. You're saying that Joe's passion for Jesus is like fire in its intensity. Just one or two features of fire are in your mind. You're not saying that Joe's passion for Jesus is like fire in its potential for destruction or its usefulness for cooking meat.

Metaphor Mania

"For some reason, metaphorical language often seems to inspire us to violate this rule. When we are told that something is 'like X,' something in us longs to stuff X full of everything we know about it. We need to fight this urge. Jesus said, 'you are the salt of the earth.' He did not mean to suggest that everything that is true about salt is true of us. It does not matter that the readers knew a hundred different things about salt. What I want to know is which of the things they knew about salt did Jesus have in mind. The context is the only way I can answer that. I have got to get control of runaway background-itis before I start saying things like:

> Fact #63 about salt: saltwater leaves a white deposit behind when it evaporates. And we, too, when we die and 'evaporate' from this world, should leave behind a deposit of good works."[32]

The author's intent always rules. Jesus said, "But I tell you who hear me: Love your enemies, do good to those who hate you, bless those who curse you, pray for those who mistreat you" (Luke 6:27-28). It's important not to "spiritualize" these words so that they mean something less challenging than Jesus intended them to mean. You take them literally. "If someone strikes you on one cheek, turn to him the other also. If someone takes your cloak, do not stop him from taking your tunic" (Luke 6:29). Again, to take Jesus literally is to figure out what He meant to say here. Was He exaggerating to make a point and disrupt His hearers' complacency? Was He laying down narrow rules about hitting and theft? Was He referring to a Jewish law regarding taking someone's cloak in a financial transaction? Was He illustrating a heart attitude that should permeate a disciple's approach to relationships? The question isn't, "What meaning would make me comfortable?" but rather "What meaning did Jesus probably intend?"

There's no virtue in being literal (non-figurative) when the biblical writer didn't intend it. Jesus warned His disciples, "Watch out for the yeast of the Pharisees and that of Herod" (Mark 8:15). They took "yeast" literally and assumed He was scolding them for forgetting to bring bread on their journey. He couldn't believe they could be so thickheaded! "Why are you talking about having no bread? Do you still not see or understand? Are your hearts hardened? Do you have eyes but fail to see, and ears but fail to hear?" (Mark 8:17-18).

How Do I Connect Old Texts to My Life?

Therefore everyone who hears these words of mine and puts them into practice is like a wise man who built his house on the rock. The rain came down, the streams rose, and the winds blew and beat against that house; yet it did not fall, because it had its foundation on the rock.

Matthew 7:24-25

Think worldview.

When you seek to build your life on Scripture, the first thing to remember is, *Think worldview.* You're not looking for a verse that will tell you what to do. You're reading the Bible in order to see the world through God's eyes. If you can see your life from God's perspective, then you're likely to respond the way God would like you to. (For more on **worldview,** see page 21.)

Worldview (heart) ➔ Values (heart) ➔ Feelings and Behavior

There are some black-and-white situations for which the Bible has simple rules about what to do. Should you have an affair with your friend's spouse? The Bible has a simple rule for this question. However, most situations are messy. Furthermore, while God is interested in your correct behavior toward your friend, God is even more concerned about what's going on in your head and your life that you would even consider this affair to be a live option. Thirdly, many of the Bible's instructions are general:

"Love your neighbor as yourself." This command is so profound and broad that you'll need an enlarged worldview to see all your opportunities to obey it today.

You can bridge from then to now because God's nature never changes.

To aid you in seeing the world through God's eyes, the Bible allows you to eavesdrop on God interacting with hundreds of people in a wide variety of situations. Your question will continually be, "If God said or did this in response to them in their situation, what does this tell me about what God would say or do in response to me in mine?"

You can bridge from then to now because God's nature never changes. His personality and values are the same as they were three thousand years ago. On the other hand, human cultures and situations do change, so you can't automatically assume that everything God said to Israel applies to you directly.

Hence, seeing your life through God's eyes involves several steps:

- Read the Scriptures to understand what the writer intended to say to his original audience. This is called the *meaning* of the text.
- Look for the *timeless issues* behind the time-limited situation the writer is addressing.
- Look for the *principles* that emerge from the way the author addresses those timeless issues.
- Think about the ways in which modern life or your personal situation are like the situation addressed in the passage. This is a *bridge* from then to now.
- Apply the principles to your modern situation. This is called the *significance* of the text for you.

(For more on **meaning and significance,** see page 82.)

This sounds abstract, but you've gone through this process thousands of times. When you were six years old, you were learning to see the world through the eyes of the primary adults in your world, probably your parents. Sometimes they gave you direct instructions, but often you watched and listened as they interacted with other people.

Let's say you had a sister named Leslie. One day, you heard your mother tell Leslie, "Don't go out in the snow without your boots on." Later, when you got ready to go outside, you may have opened the door and seen snow. If you were unbelievably smart, you went through the following reasoning so fast that you didn't notice the process:

- Mom intended Leslie to wear her boots when she walked in the snow. This was the *meaning* of Mom's words to Leslie.

- This business of snow and boots could relate to the *timeless issues* of weather and clothes. Mom has addressed these issues over and over at other times.

- Mom's words may reflect a *narrow principle:* "Wear boots when there is snow." They could display a *broader principle:* "Wear the right clothes to protect your body in each kind of weather."

- The *bridge* from my situation to Leslie's is that we both have feet that can get wet, and in both cases there is snow. Mom is consistent. Her values and personality don't change irrationally, and she often wants me to deal with weather and clothes in the same way as Leslie.

- I think Mom would want me to put on my boots before I go out. This is the *significance* of Mom's words for me.

Of course, if you were like most six-year-olds, you may have taken a wrong turn in one of these steps and come up with a significance that Mom would never have intended. Or you may have ignored Mom's words to Leslie and done what you pleased. Still, if you were committed to seeing the world through Mom's eyes, by the time you were fourteen or fifteen you may have gotten the idea about wearing boots in the snow.

Note that there's a logic to this process. There's a rational connection between the meaning of Mom's words and the significance you attach to them for yourself. If you said, "The significance for me is that running in the snow is great fun," you'd have left Mom's words far behind. You'd no longer be applying her words to your life; you'd be following your own muse.

The aim of connecting the Scriptures to your life is to arrive at God's heart for you. God is not interested in fencing you in with rules: "No boots, no snow." Life is not a power struggle with a controlling Parent. God wants to equip you with the right "clothing" to venture fearlessly and safely into the wide world in all kinds of weather.

Here are three challenges of reasoning through from a passage's meaning to its significance:

- Seeing the timeless issues in a passage is a skill. It requires some thinking. You can develop it over time.
- Drawing good principles is also a skill.
- Your situation is often different in many ways from the situation in the Bible. You may be facing mud. Mud is like snow in some ways but different in others. If Mom said Leslie needed boots for snow, what would she say about mud? So finding the bridge from then to now is another skill.

A Few Timeless Issues

Poverty
Possessions
Cultural diversity
Evangelism
Success
Human life
Physical death
How to be reconciled to God
Walls between God's people
Trust in God
Dependence on the Spirit
Fear vs. faith
Hope
Love

Seek consistency.

In order to absorb Mom's total worldview, you observed her words and actions in a range of situations over time. Eventually, you may have decided to disregard some aspects of her worldview regarding clothes. That's fine because Mom is not God. However, if God is God, then His worldview in all areas is the most consistent and true to reality that any worldview could be. It's the one that will optimize your life according to God's values, which are the best values.

This idea—that God's views are the most reality-based and His values are the best—may not yet be totally convincing to you at a gut level. You're used to thinking your views and values are just fine. You may not believe anybody has the right to claim His views are "best." This is a worldview issue. If you're struggling with it, take some time to read the Bible, trying to see the world through God's eyes. Be open with Him about your skepticism that He knows better than you. Give Him a chance to persuade you through the Scriptures and your experiences. God is not threatened by people who wrestle with Him forthrightly.

> When we "apply" what we learn in the Bible, we are seeking to rebuild our view of reality into one that is more accurate and consistent.[33]

Because God is rational and consistent, principles about God's worldview must be consistent. Consistency means that if you could fully understand everything God says and does and everything about the universe, it would all fit together in a coherent worldview. Consistency doesn't rule out mystery and paradox because you'll never fully see things from God's point of view. The Scriptures portray God as all-powerful and perfectly loving, yet He allows children to die of cancer—this is mysterious. The Scriptures describe God as being sovereign over everything that happens yet treating people as though their choices count—this is paradox. The search for consistent, coherent principles, then, is not the drive to control life by having simple answers to every question. However, seeking consistency will keep you from putting together an approach to life where what you do on Thursday contradicts what you said you believed on Sunday. God is mysterious and creative, but He is also rational and reliable.

In a complex world of competing values, *consistent principles from the Scriptures help you weigh those values the way God does.* For example, in Exodus 20:13, God commands Israel, "You shall not murder." What could be more straightforward than this command? Yet it leaves open the question, "What kinds of killing count as murder, and what kinds don't?" A study on the Hebrew word for "murder" here won't help you too much. Instead, you'll need to look at the range of cases in the Bible when God sanctions killing and when He doesn't. God actually commanded the Israelites to kill specific people for specific reasons a fair amount in the Old Testament. In order to derive principles, you'll need to pay attention to those reasons.

Then you turn to the New Testament. An interesting piece of data is that God never commands killing in the New Testament. Instead, you'll read a lot about not retaliating against evildoers. Once you have all this data, you'll create principles that link it together into a coherent whole. Did God command killing only in the limited case of Israel, or are there timeless features of a situation when killing would be right?

Here are some principles you might come up with:

- God places an enormous value on human life.
- God places an enormous value on justice.
- In the Old Testament, sometimes God's love of justice takes a higher priority than His concern for physical life, so He instructs His people to kill other people who have done wrong. This happens quite a bit in the Old Testament but never in the New Testament.
- God is very concerned about the misuse of human anger. When human anger leads to violence, God often condemns this as sin. God highly values non-destructive ways of handling anger.
- God highly values people's coming to faith in Christ.
- In the New Testament, believers are expressly warned against trying to spread the gospel through violence. Here, God's value of conversion does not take a higher priority than His value of human life.
- God values responding to evil with good.
- God values forgiveness.

Notice that these principles reflect competing values (human life, justice, forgiveness, the spread of the gospel) and that *God has a coherent worldview by which He decides which value is higher in a given situation.* When you get used to observing how God weighs values in various situations, you'll have a coherent lens through which to see modern situations involving war, punishing criminals, abortion, and self-defense. Forming principles "makes it possible to release a command from a particular set of circumstances and allow it to inform actions in a completely different set of circumstances."[34]

Balance breadth and depth.

The more of the Bible you read with understanding, the fuller will be your view of life through God's eyes. Take the topic of money, for example. How does God view money? You can read the Old Testament narratives to see God dealing with rich people, poor people, greedy people, and generous people. You can read the laws about money that God gave to the nation of Israel. The Prophets gave us God's unvarnished opinions about how the Israelites were handling money. The proverbs offer practical wisdom on money management. Jesus talked a lot about money. So did Paul. Taken together, this material will tell you not only that God thinks money is an extremely important spiritual issue, but also how He views the array of ways in which people use it. (For more on **reading for breadth,** see page 70.)

In fact, the Bible contains so much material on money that you'll need time to absorb it. Learning the information is not the same as see-ing life through God's eyes. You'll need to choose a pace of study and reflection that enables you to understand at a heart level what's being said, see timeless truths, form principles, and build bridges to your situation. There's no written exam; the true test will be to see how you're actually handling money a year later. Therefore, you may need to slow down and take one passage at a time. Chew on it until you "get it," whether that takes a few hours or a month. It's usually best to start with something from the New Testament. Don't take a single verse out of context: Be sure you understand the words of Jesus or the apostles in the context of several paragraphs or a chapter. Then meditate

A Few Principles About Money

God owns everything.

God entrusts possessions to people to be used for His kingdom purposes.

God is especially concerned about the poor.

Hard work and sober living will usually pay off.

Families are expected to take care of their members.

God hates envy of others' possessions.

Greed is worship of a false god and is destructive.

Greed and envy are pointless: God takes care of His own.

on the story or teaching until it's part of you. (For more on **reading for depth,** see page 71.)

Don't ignore your experience.

A child gathers information by watching and listening to his mother. He also learns by interacting with his environment. He tries things, and the world responds. That's how he finds out that you can fall down stairs, that stoves are sometimes hot, and that ice cream tastes good.

In the same way, your insights from the Bible will be pointless unless you're engaged both with the Bible and your experience. The goal is to build a worldview that makes sense of your experience of reality and your interpretation of Scripture.

Experience Plus Scripture

"Because we have seen so many people misunderstand their experience, we Christians tend to be suspicious of experience itself. It is fair to conclude that we must be careful when we analyze experience, but we ought not conclude that experience itself is unreliable. Many people misapply the Bible, but do we assume that the defect is in the Bible itself? Of course not. Therefore, when people misunderstand their experience, we should realize that the source of the problem lies not in the experience, but in the interpretation of that experience. . . .

"When our interpretation of reality does not match our understanding of Scripture we should not conclude that Scripture is in error, nor should we conclude that reality is in error. Both Scripture and reality are accurate revelations from God; they both testify to the same truth; therefore, they must be consistent. If we find apparent discrepancies between Scripture and reality then we have misunderstood something; each is a check on the other."[35]

According to Romans 1:20, God's eternal power and divine nature can be accurately seen from experience. That's why people who have never seen a Bible are accountable for their beliefs about God. So experience is valuable; the problem is the eyeglasses or worldview through which people interpret experience.

For example, a woman named Marta might reach the age of forty and evaluate her experience like this: "I'm not married. Being single and childless is painful. I could have avoided this pain if I had married Jeff. Jeff broke up with me because I wouldn't move in with him without being married. It was a mistake to be so rigid about the Bible's sexual standards. I would be happy now if I had seen that those standards are outmoded in today's world." You can see that Marta's interpretation of her experience and the Bible is filtered through some questionable worldview assumptions, such as:

- Marta believes the point of life is to minimize pain. Is that true? What does God think about that?
- Marta thinks married people are happier than single ones. Does the Bible have any evidence on that?
- Marta thinks Jeff would have made a good husband. What are the qualities of a person likely to be a reliable partner through the trials of life? What could Marta learn about this from the Bible?

Marta doesn't need to throw out her experience and just listen to the Bible. She also doesn't need to throw out the Bible and learn only from experience. She needs to go to the Bible with questions prompted by experience and rethink her experience in light of the Bible.

So if your interpretation of reality conflicts with your interpretation of Scripture, you know one is wrong. In order to connect Scripture to your life, you'll need to go back and examine both experience and Scripture more closely. Input from other people can help you get past your blind spots.

In some cases you may never fully understand your experience. When a child dies, a parent may never fully understand how the scriptural teaching that God is good can be consistent with the experience of this loss. This is mystery. But the fact that the parent can never fully understand the consistency between Scripture and experience doesn't mean there is no consistency. Nor does it mean the parent won't grow from struggling to see the consistency, the goodness of God at work in the midst of suffering.

Aim for heart growth, not mechanical obedience.

There are times when you just have to pull yourself together and obey a command of Scripture. You don't feel like it; you just do it because you know it's right. In these cases, your feelings will often come around eventually.

However, "just do it" is not the standard slogan for living by the Book. For one thing, a mechanical "just do it" attitude doesn't equip you to respond to the range of situations life will throw at you. "Love your neighbor as yourself." Fine, but what is the loving way to deal with this particular neighbor? Jesus was endlessly creative in His loving responses to unique individuals. He never dealt with two people in the same way. Jesus' *principles* were consistent, but because they added up to seeing the world from God's perspective, He could be creative and flexible without abandoning standards.

Second, if your heart is too small, you may not have the capacity to "just do it" when "it" is a command like "clothe yourselves with compassion, kindness, humility, gentleness and patience. Bear with each other and forgive whatever grievances you may have against one another" (Colossians 3:12-13). Obeying a command like this takes a process of living in partnership with the Holy Spirit as your personal trainer. (For more on the **spirit as your personal trainer,** see page 65.)

God's commands always burrow to the core of who you are. The Bible uses the word *heart* for the source of your motives, values, desires, passions, will, and deepest beliefs. Just as you need well-developed lungs to run marathons, you need a well-developed heart to value flawed and broken people robustly. It's not that difficult for most men to avoid adultery but to treat every woman as a person rather than an object requires a well-developed heart (Matthew 5:27-28). It's not that hard to avoid murder but criticism and putdowns are tougher (Matthew 5:21-22). Sticking to the letter of a contract is far simpler than being consistently true to your word

(Matthew 5:33-37). You can see why Jesus said His followers' righteousness must exceed that of the admirable religious people of His day, whose mechanical obedience to God's commands was undeniable (Matthew 5:17-20).

You Know You're Off-track If. . .

1. You notice only the Bible's comforting words. Yes, God wants to calm your anxiety and unburden you from guilt. You live in an utterly safe universe run by an unimaginably good God who offers you total forgiveness through the shed blood of Christ. Nevertheless, this God also wants to expose your blind spots and draw you to take risks for those who need your love and faith. Make an effort to deliberately notice things in the Bible that challenge your comfortable world.

2. You notice only the Bible's critical words. God is often scathing toward sinners. There's a lot of wrath and rebuke in the Bible. Yet if you can't open the Scriptures without feeling ashamed of how far short you fall of God's standards, you're screening out the good news. Meditate on John 8:1-11 or Romans 8:28-39.

3. The Bible always reinforces what you already believed about life. Unless you already see the world perfectly as God does, at least once a year you should realize, "Wow, I was wrong."

Take the long view.

The process of building a worldview like God's will take your whole life. You'll need humility because you'll continually have to realize that you haven't been seeing things clearly enough. You'll continually update your understanding of how God looks at things when you read a new Bible passage, when an experience pushes you back to an old passage again, or when you learn new background about a passage.

"Face the book with a new attitude as something new. . . . You do not know which of its sayings and images will overwhelm and mold you."

Martin Buber[1]

What Can I Learn from
Old Testament
History?

*These things
happened to them
as examples
and were written
down as warnings
for us, on whom
the fulfillment
of the ages
has come.*

1 Corinthians 10:11

Some people have no interest in history. Why wallow in the past? What matters is the present and the future!

But most of the Bible is written in the form of history. The biblical writers recount the past precisely in order to equip you for the present and the future. The historical books of the Old Testament explain what God did in the past so you can understand what God is doing now and will do in years to come.

How does God act?

The doctrinal sections of Scripture make statements about God: God is love; God is holy. But what does it mean to say that God is love? Is

---

**Books of Old
Testament History**

Genesis
Exodus (portions)
Leviticus (portions)
Numbers (portions)
Deuteronomy (portions)
Joshua, Judges, Ruth
1 & 2 Samuel
1 & 2 Kings
1 & 2 Chronicles
Ezra, Nehemiah, Esther
Isaiah, Jeremiah, Ezekiel,
Daniel (portions)

God just the spirit of warm feelings? Old Testament history puts meat on those abstract bones. The histories are written for people who want to see God in action, showing what He means by love, holiness, justice, faithfulness, and so on.

The histories present the Ultimate acting within space and time—the same space and time you inhabit. The Israelites in Egypt were humans like you—they ate and slept, got sick, felt pain, bled and sweated, felt hope and fear, hated going hungry, wanted sex and children, felt grief when people died—they were human. Exodus 2:25 says God saw these people suffering and "was concerned about them."[2] That is, God didn't just observe from a distance. He connected. He felt, and He acted. The events of Exodus actually happened in a place and time as real as the one you live in.

God doesn't change over time, so you can expect Him to love the same things, hate the same things, want the same things, and take action on the same scale throughout history.

> ### Exercise
>
> Read one of the history books, asking yourself:
> • How does God act with love, justice, mercy, power, or wisdom in this story?
> • What is my life like if this is the God who is active in my world?

If God did it then, why doesn't He do it now?

You may wonder, if God is the same now as He was then, why don't I see Him doing miracles the way He did in the Old Testament? If you look around and don't see rivers turned to blood or lepers healed instantly, you may conclude that the Old Testament stories are just inspiring legends.

The first thing to remember is that in the Bible, the special effects were not the main show. God performed them to serve the plot (His plan) and the characters (Himself and His people). He used the flashy stuff sparingly, at key moments, to move events or to make a point about Himself or His kingdom.

Throughout most of history and prehistory, God has preferred to let the laws of physics, chemistry, and biology—which He invented—play out naturally. It's easy to lose sight of this fact when you read the Bible because the biblical writers skipped over those vast stretches of time and focused on strategic moments when God entered history. For example, God allowed generations of humans in the Middle East to figure out how to plant crops and herd goats, invent writing, fight wars, kidnap women and kill babies, die of diseases or live to see their grandchildren. Then out of the blue, God spoke to a particular Iraqi herdsman named Abram and began to direct this man's life (Genesis 12). Meanwhile, thousands of people in Africa went on hunting game in the jungle and across the plains without any idea that the Creator of the universe was up to something in the Middle East.

God sent Moses and a series of dramatic plagues to Egypt for a strategic reason: to liberate the descendants of Abraham from slavery so they could play a key role in His plan for the world. When you read the story of the Exodus and wonder about the miracles, remember:

- The God of the Exodus is the God of today. He still opposes the oppressor and cares for the oppressed. He wants you to share those values.

- In nations today where people are being oppressed, God can intervene just as dramatically. He can send prophets or plagues. There is nothing inherently different about now that prevents this.

- It is entirely appropriate for oppressed people to cry out to God just as the Israelites did in Egypt. It's appropriate for God's people to ask Him to intervene.

- God can use exactly the same methods for accomplishing His ends, but He doesn't have to. He can do something flashy, or He can act covertly through people or events that appear ordinary.

- God can call anybody to lead the effort. There was nothing inherently unique about Moses. Moses was human. God gave him an assignment. God could give you an assignment.

- While liberating oppressed people is an important value to God, the Exodus was a unique event. God intervened dramatically for this particular oppressed people because He had a long-range plan for global liberation. His ultimate goal is not to have to send in the Marines for every suffering group in every country in every generation. As long as sin persists, powerful people are going to exploit weaker people. God's long-range plan is to wipe out sin.

Maybe liberation for an oppressed people is not at the front of your mind. Maybe you're more interested in the personal miracles, such as the healings performed by Elisha and Elijah in 1 and 2 Kings. Those were on the minds of the citizens of Nazareth, Jesus' hometown, when He visited there after doing a streak of miracles in a neighboring village:

> Jesus said to them, "Surely you will quote this proverb to me: 'Physician, heal yourself! Do here in your hometown what we have heard that you did in Capernaum.'"

> "I assure you that there were many widows in Israel in Elijah's time, when the sky was shut for three and a half years and there was a severe famine throughout the land. Yet Elijah was not sent to any of them, but to a widow in Zarephath in the region of Sidon. And there were many in Israel with leprosy in the time of Elisha the prophet, yet not one of them was cleansed—only Naaman the Syrian." (Luke 4:23-27)

Jesus pointed out that Elijah did only a handful of miracles in his long prophetic career, and God chose to do one of the big ones not in Israel but in a foreign country. Likewise, Elisha did just a few healings, and the main one was for a foreigner. Miracles were not the focus of these prophets' ministries. Miracles were lessons—illustrations—not ends in themselves. To seek the miracle rather than God Himself is to miss the point tragically. The people of Nazareth lost the chance to experience God in the flesh because they were so intent upon relief for their physical aches.

Therefore, when you read about miraculous healings in the Bible, remember:

- God is the same today as He was in the time of Elijah or Jesus. He can do miraculous healings whenever and wherever He chooses.
- God still hates suffering—even the suffering of people who live far away from you—and wants you to have the same values.
- It is completely appropriate to ask God to heal you or someone you love. God is a loving Parent and is happy for you to ask for anything and every-

thing. God may say yes. And even if God doesn't say yes (as good parents often don't), He still is committed to good in your life.

- If God doesn't heal your loved one, there's no scriptural evidence that there's something wrong with God or with you.
- If God isn't doing healing miracles in your church or your life, but is doing them in another town or another country, that's well within the biblical pattern. That may be exactly what God intends. Of course, there's the possibility that you or your church are blocking God's grace by a faithlessness like that of Nazareth. But note that the problem in Nazareth was not that people didn't believe Jesus could do miracles. The problem was that they wanted miracles but didn't want the real Jesus Himself.
- It's not God's plan to miraculously heal every individual who is prayed for. God's plan is bigger than that. He is tirelessly at work on His long-range plan, which includes abolishing disease and death.

Like the citizens of Nazareth, too many modern people read biblical history through the filter of "What's in it for me?" Individualism and self-centeredness are part of the modern worldview that God wants to correct. (For more on **individualism,** see page 21. For more on **self-centeredness,** see page 38.) If you tend toward that way of thinking, try to read the Old Testament stories, especially the miraculous ones, with questions like:

- How does this story show God's care for an individual?
- How does it show God's care for His chosen people?
- How does it show God's care for all the nations of the world?
- How does this miracle contribute to God's plan to redeem the world?

At the same time, avoid the tendency to tell yourself, "That could never happen to me." It could.

> *Elijah was a man just like us. He prayed earnestly that it would not rain, and it did not rain in the land for three and a half years. Again he prayed, and the heavens gave rain, and the earth produced its crops.* (James 5:17-18)

James told his readers to pray with the confidence that God was just as likely to say yes to them as to Elijah. There was nothing special about Elijah except that he decided to get serious about God. He was a normal human. He got scared. He got burnt out. He had ups and downs. Anything that happened to Elijah could happen to you. God could talk to you just as He did to Elijah or do miracles through you in the same way.

Real People, Just Like You

"Conversely, if we are really to understand the Bible record, we must enter into our study of it on the assumption that the experiences recorded there are basically of the same type as ours would have been if we had been there. Those who lived through those experiences felt very much as we would have if we had been in their place. Unless this comes home to us, the things that happened to the people in the Bible will remain unreal to us. We will not genuinely be able to believe the Bible or find its contents to be real, because it will have no experiential substance for us.

"Failure to read the Bible in this realistic manner accounts for two common problems in Christian groups that hold the Bible central to their faith. One is that it becomes simply a book of doctrine, of abstract truth about God, in which one can search endlessly without encountering God himself or hearing his voice."[3]

What is the main point of the history books?

If the special effects aren't the main point of the history books, what is? To answer this question, look at two features that every story has (whether it's true or made up, ancient or modern): character and plot.[4]

Characters.

In the Bible, God is always the main character. God is always the Hero, and the humans play supporting roles. (For more on **God as hero,** see page 27.) It's easy to lose sight of this fact because the human characters are so interesting and because one can identify with David or Ruth more readily than with God.

The human characters are not irrelevant, and you can learn a lot from studying them. However, one thing you'll learn is that their faith and effectiveness were directly proportional to their awareness that *they were not the heroes of their own stories.* For example, as a young man, Moses was horrified at the way the Egyptian government was oppressing the Hebrews. He tried to play the hero in this situation—with disastrous results. He killed someone and had to flee the country. Years later, he started taking orders from God. He led the people's successful liberation from slavery, and after that he was almost always careful to let God call the shots and take the top billing He deserved. Just once, Moses slipped. In a moment of annoyance, he acted as though he were the one responsible for taking care of the people. He "adapted" one of God's instructions to make the scene more dramatic and himself the star. This incident cost him the chance to be in the limelight when the people entered the Promised Land (Numbers 20:1-13).

This focus on God should put your ego into perspective. Moses was a talented guy, no question. But fundamentally, he was nobody special. Signing on with God's plan was what enabled him to do something special. Joshua was just as capable of leading the Israelites into the Promised Land—he did it. And Joshua was nobody special. It could just as easily have been you if you had been there, had been willing to do whatever job God assigned to you, and had resisted the temptation to sign autographs.

Studying a Human Character

Even though God is the Hero of all the Bible's stories, you can still profit from studying the human characters. Here are some pointers for doing character study:

- Choose a biblical person to study.
- Use your reference tools to find all the places in the Bible where that person is mentioned. You can look up her name in a concordance and check the cross-reference column in your Bible. (For more on **resources,** see page 105.)
- Read so that this character comes alive for you. He was a real person, as human as you are. When and where did he live? What was going on in the world at that time? What can you learn about his family? What did he do for a living? What did he eat, drink, do for fun? How would you describe his personality? What was his heart attitude toward God? How did his relationship with God grow or not grow over time? How, if at all, did he serve God? What was important to him? What were his likes and dislikes? How did he relate to other people? What did he think about? What feelings did he show? How did he hurt? How did he die? You won't be able to find answers to all of these questions for every character, but these will spark your thinking.
- Think about the bigger picture. Why did the biblical writer(s) tell this person's story? How does she fit into the larger story the writer is telling?
- Evaluate the character's behavior. He's human, so even if he's generally a godly person, not everything he does is admirable or worthy of imitation. When does he shine? When does he blow it?
- Remember that God is the Hero. How does God interact with this person's life?
- Look for connections between your life and the character's. In what ways is your story like her story? In what ways is it different? How would you compare your values, hopes, fears, and desires?
- Pray about the character's story and your story. What could God be telling you about yourself through this person's life? What could God be calling you to do?

Plot.

At the highest level, a single plot or story line runs throughout the history books—in fact, throughout the Scriptures. That story line is God's plan to redeem the world through the descendants of Abraham—and eventually through one descendant in particular. (For more on **God's plan,** see page 28.)

God's Plan

"God is sovereign and in control of history. Not only is He all-powerful and all-knowing about the events of history, He is also initiating and working out *His plan* for human history. . . . [The history books] declare in story after story and event after event that God is the shaper of history. He is not removed, nor uninvolved, nor silent. He is not surprised by human choices or mortal actions. He is ultimately in control of this world and the next. Additionally, God does have both a sense and a scenario of where history is going and where it will end. He ordained it; He planned it; He will bring it to the completion and fruition that He desires. . . . Moreover, in the narratives and histories of the Old Testament, God co-labors with His people through events far worse than those in the morning paper. For example, consider the catastrophic loss of life, moral crises, political turmoil, and consequent economic collapse connected with the fall of Jerusalem in 2 Kings 25. . . . We can be confident that God is working out a plan in human history because only a defined plan could survive the catastrophic collapse and exile of God's people! . . . Only a God-ordained plan in history could give meaning to such malevolent and terrifying evils as Jeremiah recounts in Lamentations. . . . Finally, God's plan for history is, at its core, a plan to bless, not curse, the people of planet earth."[5]

The New Testament explains how God redeemed a people for Himself through Christ, and how He's working out His plan to bring the whole universe together under the benevolent reign of Christ. But this plan did not spring from nowhere on the day the angel told Mary she was pregnant. Old Testament history reveals why the plan was necessary, how God launched it as soon as Adam and Eve first rebelled against Him, and how He nurtured it through the centuries until the time was ripe. Understanding Old Testament history helps you make sense of the New Testament.

The history books of the Old and New Testaments have three levels of plot:[6]

The top level: God's universal plan worked out through the created universe. Key plot points include:

- The creation of the world
- Humanity's fall into sin
- The power of sin in every individual and human institution
- The need for redemption
- Christ's incarnation, sacrifice, and resurrection

The mid-level: Israel, the church, and their role in God's plan. Key plot points include:

- The call of Abraham
- The establishment of a covenant people through Abraham's descendants (Isaac, Jacob)
- The enslavement of the covenant people in Egypt
- Freedom from slavery by God's intervention
- Conquest of the Promised Land
- Israel's frequent rebellion against God
- God's patient pursuit of and protection for Israel in the face of repeated rejection
- The destruction of the northern kingdom of Israel
- Judah's destruction and the exile in Babylon
- The restoration of the covenant people in the Promised Land after the exile
- Continued sin and continued subjection to foreign domination
- The arrival of the Messiah Jesus
- The rejection of the Messiah by most of the heirs of the Old Covenant (Jews)
- The birth of a new configuration of a covenant people—Jews and Gentiles—under a new covenant

The bottom level: Individual stories that make up the higher levels. Key plot points include:

- Abraham offering his son Isaac as a sacrifice to God
- David defeating Goliath

Top Level Questions

What is God doing in the world?

How does this story help me understand what God is doing?

How can I participate in what God is doing?

Mid-Level Questions

Who am I as part of God's people?

What is our heritage?

How can I participate in what we are about?

What mistakes have we, God's people, made in the past?

How can I contribute to our avoiding repetition of those mistakes?

Bottom Level Questions

What were this character's positive and negative qualities?

How am I like or unlike this character?

How can I use this character as a role model for my individual life?

The modern Western worldview is individualistic. It treats the individual as more important than the community or God. Viewing the world through this lens, most people today are interested in the bottom level of the biblical story because it deals with individuals. In past centuries, when people got their identity from belonging to a group, they were more interested in the story of God's people. Even today, in cultures with more of a group orientation, people are more attuned to this bigger picture.

There's nothing wrong with looking to the Bible's history books for individual role models. However, if you tend to do this exclusively, try reading for the larger story. Just as one scene in a movie is most important for the way it contributes to the whole movie, so one story about David is most important for what it says about the growth of Israel or the working out of God's plan. The best way to gain value from Bible characters as role models is to do what they did: look beyond them to the larger story.

Shifting your focus to the larger story in this way will spiral you up and out of your personal problems.

The larger story will keep you from being tyrannized by the problems or pleasures of your personal life. Let's say your job is frustrating and your closest relationships aren't all you'd like them to be. Problems like these can dominate your mood. If you read the story of Abraham or Esther and focus on them as individuals, you might ask yourself, "Why can't I have Abraham's faith or Esther's courage? Why can't my life work out as well as theirs did?" If you're already preoccupied with your personal struggles, focusing on these individuals can make you spiral further into yourself. On the other hand, think what happens when you take on Abraham's or Esther's worldview: Abraham developed faith by acknowledging God as the star of his story. His life was meaningful because he entered into the larger story of what God was doing in the world. Likewise, Esther acted bravely despite her fear because she was convinced that there were more important things on earth than her private safety. She treated God's people and God's plan as worth the risk of her individual life. Shifting your focus to the larger story in this way will spiral you up and out of your personal problems. No matter what happens in your job or relationships, you are still part of God's people and can contribute to God's plan.

Awareness of the larger story can also keep you from being misled when Bible characters behave badly. The Scriptures present even the big names—Abraham, Moses, David—as flawed humans. The Holy Spirit may not have intended them as shining examples of how to behave. In fact, He may have intended them as proof that God can accomplish His plan even through people with major limitations. Take Gideon, for example. God wanted to rescue His people, and He wanted to do it in a way that would leave no doubt that God, not a human warrior, deserved the credit. So He chose Gideon, who by his own admission was the most insignificant member of an insignificant clan (Judges 6:15). Gideon didn't believe he was really hearing from God, so to get out of the job, he gave God a series of dares: if you're really God, do something supernatural. These dares involved a sheepskin or "fleece." Because Gideon ended up fighting and winning the battle, some readers of Judges have assumed that setting tests or "fleeces" for God is a model God wants them to imitate. Even though Jesus said putting God to the test was wrong (Matthew 4:7), the temptation to make a role model of Gideon is strong. But Gideon is not given to you as a role model any more than promiscuous Samson or Ehud who assassinated the king of Moab. None of them were people you'd go to for spiritual advice. Instead, the Holy Spirit provided their stories as part of the larger story of God protecting His people through a dark and violent era.

Gideon is not given to you as a role model.

Of course, it's just as easy to misuse the top and mid-level of Old Testament history. The conquest of the Promised Land has often appealed to Christians who have felt as persecuted as the Israelites. When devout Dutch Reformed Christians fled Holland for South Africa several hundred years ago, they were convinced that God had given them the southern tip of Africa as their Promised Land. They applied the book of Joshua to their situation. Accordingly, they viewed the native population as pagan Canaanites whom they were supposed to wipe out or subdue. This conviction was the theological core that enabled good, God-fearing Christians to support the brutal apartheid regime in South Africa right up until the end of the twentieth century. They genuinely believed God had commanded them to treat the nonwhites in South Africa as Canaanites. They were utterly sincere, and sincerely wrong. They didn't understand that "holy war" was a unique, one-time event when God's people were concentrated in one ethnic group.

Your best protection against making a huge mistake like that is to admit that you're capable of it. All of us are capable of reading an appealing Bible story and assuming it's about us. Let the whopping mistakes of Christian history motivate you to know God's Word well enough to avoid getting yourself caught up in whatever the next whopper turns out to be.

What Can I Learn from Old Testament Law?

> "Do not think I have come to abolish the Law or the Prophets; I have not come to abolish them but to fulfill them. I tell you the truth, until heaven and earth disappear, not the smallest letter, not the least stroke of a pen, will by any means disappear from the Law until everything is accomplished."
>
> Matthew 5:17-18

"Commands become outdated, but they are never irrelevant. . . . A command is always addressed to a specific person or group of persons in a specific situation."[7]

A quarterback orders a play. He gives instructions to a wide receiver. This command applies to that specific player in that specific play. What if the wide receiver assumes he should do exactly the same thing in every play in every game? He's misunderstood the point of the command. What if the whole team does what the wide receiver was told to do? Again, the quarterback is not being understood and properly obeyed. His instructions were addressed to a specific person in a specific situation.

A new player joins the team. Is it worth his while to study the plays the quarterback called in previous games? Are those commands relevant to him? Not in the sense that he's supposed to do exactly what the quarterback told the wide receiver weeks ago. But studying those plays can tell him a lot about how the quarterback's mind works, his personality, the

Books of Law
Exodus
Leviticus
Numbers
Deuteronomy

approach to the game he values, and what he doesn't like. Those old plays can help him see the game through the quarterback's eyes, and that will help him contribute more effectively to the team. In some cases, the quarterback will repeat an old play, and the new player will be prepared.

In the same way, the Law was God's instruction book to the ethnic nation of Israel for a specific time and situation. Some things about "the game" (life, God's ongoing work of redeeming the world) and "the team" (God's people) have changed. Some things are much the same as they were three thousand years ago. As a new player, you can learn a lot from both what's changed and what hasn't.

The Law will help you understand the connection between God's grace and your obedience.

The Jews refer to the first five books of the Bible as the Torah. This Hebrew word is usually translated as "the Law." However, all of Genesis and large portions of the other four books of Torah are history. The Jewish Law is embedded in the history of how God chose the family of Abraham and built it into a nation.

This fact tells you that God's commands have *always* been rooted in His loving call. Obedience to His commands has *always* been a response to His grace, never a condition of earning His grace. Even the famous Ten Commandments begin,

> *"I am the LORD your God, who brought you out of Egypt, out of the land of slavery.*
> *"[Therefore] You shall have no other gods before me."* (Exodus 20:2-3)

First God saved a group of people from miserable slavery. Then He declared His intention to give them land, forge them into a nation, and reign as God and King over the nation. Then He made a *covenant* with them, spelling out how they would relate to each other: King to people, people to King, and people to people. A covenant is an agreement, treaty, or contract. It spells out rights and obligations of all the parties. The covenant between God and Israel was pure gift. Israel did nothing to earn liberation, a land, a just system of laws, and a just King. God gave this gift to demonstrate His love and to further His plan to bless the world through His people.

Many people today struggle with obedience. Authorities are suspect. Laws are seen as arbitrary limits on people's freedom. The fewer laws, the better. In this worldview, God can look like the cosmic Cop demanding that you earn His approval—and escape His punishment—by towing the line. But God is not the cosmic Cop. He's not your parents, your eighth-grade teacher, your high school principal, your boss, or the politicians on the evening news. If you read the Law through the lens of *grace*, of generous and unearned gift, you'll see an authority figure who is tough but honest, committed to His people's good, committed to justice, and not an egotist. Although most of the Old Testament laws aren't laws you need to obey, there are New Testament commands you do need to obey. The old sheds light on the new. God is still in this for your good and the good of all people. And your obedience is still not a way of your earning His favor but *a response to His earning your trust*. God earned Israel's trust by liberating them from Egypt. He's earned your trust by liberating you from meaninglessness, a self-focused and self-defeating life, destructive behaviors, and death. Jesus said, "If you love me, you will obey what I command" (John 14:15)—obedience has always been a response to God's love and a demonstration of our love.

The Law will help you understand justice.

The laws contained in the Law were given to ethnic Israel as a sort of constitution for that nation. They're not a comprehensive legal code covering every issue that might come up. Instead, the six-hundred-plus laws are "illustrative cases or topics whose legal principles were to serve as a guide to Israel. Their purpose was to teach the Israelites fundamental values. . ."[8] and to lay out the basic structure for the nation.

The principles and values of the Law will tell you what God means by "justice." In fact, those principles are foundational for the legal systems of Western democratic countries. For example:

- In the ancient world, family revenge was traditional. If someone beat up your brother, the men in your family would beat up and perhaps kill that person's whole family. To cut short these escalating cycles of violence, God's Law established the principle that the punishment must be proportional to the crime: "eye for eye, tooth for tooth, hand for hand. . ." (Exodus 21:24). The community, not the family, took action so that blood feuds could be avoided. Examples in other portions of Exodus made clear that "eye for eye" was a figure of speech, not a literal practice of maiming criminals.

- God's Law was also revolutionary in treating commoners' lives as equal in value to noblemen's and in protecting women and slaves from being used as property.
- Even a king was subject to God's Law.
- Brutal treatment of criminals was sharply limited compared to elsewhere in the ancient world.
- At least two witnesses were required to convict a criminal.
- Judges were forbidden to show favoritism to the rich or to allow a crowd to sway them.
- Fraud and bribery flourished in ancient times. God's Law forbade both.
- Care for the poor and foreigners was insisted upon.
- Even the farmland had to be treated wisely so it would be fertile for future generations.
- Individuals and families could accumulate private property, but a standard of ethical accumulation was set and the needs of the whole community were part of the equation.

God still hates injustice. He still wants His people to practice justice in their personal lives and work for justice in their wider communities. The Law can inspire your thinking about what justice would look like in your society.

Exercise

- Read a portion of Israel's legal code, such as Exodus 20-23.
- Which laws sound harsh to your ears? Why?
- What principles and values lie behind these laws?
- Which values do you especially admire?
- Are there any social or political issues in your country that these principles could apply to?

The Law will help you understand holiness.

First Peter 1:15 repeats the Law's command, "Be holy, because I [God] am holy" (compare Leviticus 11:44-45; 19:2; 20:7). If the word *holy* doesn't create a clear picture in your mind, the Law offers full-color graphics. God gave Israel rituals for purity in food, clothing, sexuality, worship, work, and every other area of life in order to drive home several points:

- God is radically Other. He can't be reduced to manageable proportions. Fear is a reasonable response to an encounter with God. If worship makes you yawn or just have a good time, you may not be coming face to face with the Holy Other.

- To be holy is to be set apart for God's purposes. This is a total dedication involving every detail of life. Nobody is a little holy, holy on Sundays, or holy except when it gets in the way.

- Holiness isn't just being spiritual. How you treat people is essential to holiness.

- Sin is serious business. You can't get within a million miles of God if you're carrying around the consequences of your self-centeredness. The Israelites offered substitutes for their wrongdoing until the air reeked of blood and burning carcasses. If you're so familiar with the Cross that it no longer shocks you, read Leviticus 1–10 and 16. This enormous, messy, smelly piece of theater went on for centuries so you would understand that "Jesus dying for my sins" is more than an empty phrase.

- God never expected humans to be able to keep the Law perfectly. That's why they needed the sacrificial system in the first place. You can't be holy by trying harder.

The Law's system of sacrifices, the rules about clean and unclean food and people, and all the rest of the holiness code should make you uncomfortable. Reading about God's holiness and His expectations for human holiness should send you running to the Gospels in order to be around Jesus, in whom the Holy Other became human. After you read Leviticus, Jesus' life and death are breathtaking.

What Does "Clean" Mean?

In the Law, "clean" and "unclean" have to do with ritual purity, the separation between the common and the holy. Common wasn't bad; it was just merely human or merely earthly. The cleanness rules taught Israel that even things of everyday life led a person into that boundary zone. For example, menstrual blood and semen were quintessential symbols of human life, so contact with them produced ritual uncleanness. Even eating became an exercise in holiness because foods were divided into clean and unclean.

These cleanness rituals don't apply to you. But what reminders can you scatter through your day to recall that the most mundane or unmentionable parts of your life are tinged with the presence of holiness?

The Old Covenant will help you understand the New Covenant.

Christians refer to the Law as the Old Covenant or Old Testament because it was revised when Christ came. Like treaties and contracts, covenants can be updated as circumstances change. Christ instituted the New Covenant because:

- The old one was designed for the ethnic nation of Israel, but the new one needed to work for a multiethnic international community.
- The old one lacked power to transform people's hearts so that they could live by the heart attitudes expressed in the laws.
- The sacrificial laws were fulfilled once for all time when Christ died on the cross, so they were no longer needed.
- The Old Covenant assumed the King lived separate from His people because sinful people would be consumed by His holiness. The New

Covenant makes provision for the King dwelling in the hearts of all His people through the Holy Spirit.

Many provisions of the Law were not renewed in the covenant under which you live. You don't have to burn bulls and goats in order to be forgiven for your sin (Leviticus 7:1-10). You don't have to worry about rules for haircuts that were designed for a setting where hair was used in the worship of other gods (Leviticus 19:27). You don't have to obey the civil laws that imposed crimes and penalties for the political nation of Israel.

But some aspects of the old laws were renewed in the New Covenant. An example is Leviticus 19:17-18:

> *"Do not hate your brother in your heart. Rebuke your neighbor frankly so you will not share in his guilt.*
>
> *"Do not seek revenge or bear a grudge against one of your people, but love your neighbor as yourself. I am the LORD."*

Jesus renewed these commands in Luke 10:25-37 and 17:3-4. In doing so, He expanded and adapted them to be even more generous than under the original Law. Notice that these laws involve both outward behavior and deep attitudes and desires of the heart, such as love and hatred, grudges and forgiveness.

Even the old laws that Jesus repealed highlight ways in which the New Covenant is truly new and radical. For example, some of the old laws defined customs to keep Israel distinct from neighboring nations. It was important for Israel to remain ethnically and culturally separate so that the tiny community could avoid being absorbed by the stronger nations nearby. Christ repealed these laws when He established the New Covenant because ethnic distinctiveness was no longer desirable for God's people. The book of Acts and the letters of Paul stress this change — the multiethnic, welcoming stance of the New Covenant. The better you understand why ethnic separateness was important in Israel, the better you'll understand why ethnic diversity is valuable in the church. Also, you'll see why the New Testament writers insisted God's people need to be *morally* set apart from the crowd even while their mission sends them into the world's cultures. In place of outward cleanness rituals, the New Covenant offers a process by which the Holy Spirit purifies the believer's heart. This transition from ethnic separateness to ethical uniqueness gets a lot of ink in the New Testament.

Several of the New Testament writers said strongly negative things about the Law. They did so not because the Old Covenant was bad or irrelevant (Romans 7:7-13), but because it was so important to embrace the improvements of the New Covenant. If your time is limited, devote most of it to absorbing and living by the New Covenant. But you'll find your understanding enriched if you also give some time to the Old Covenant.

> *I'm thanking you, GOD,*
> *out in the streets,*
> *singing your praises*
> *in town and country.*
>
> **Psalm 108:3 MSG**

What Can I Learn from the Psalms?

A vocabulary of passionate prayer

God summons you to love Him with all your mind. He asks you to think about heavy things like justice and holiness. Commitment, obedience—these are the bones and sinews of love.

Yet love claims also your heart and soul and strength. Walking in obedience is not enough. The Psalms invite you to run, even fly, with passion. Bring all your passions to God: joy, contentment, courage, fear, grief, fury. Are you mad at hell and can't take it anymore? The psalmists have felt like that. Are you soaring with relief that a long torment is finally over? The psalmists have been there too.

> **Exercise**
>
> Read through the Psalms, looking for vocabulary you can use to express your own thoughts and feelings to God. Find a psalm you can pray when you're angry, one for when you're scared, one for grief, one for discouragement, and several for gratitude and joy. Mark or copy these passages so you'll have them when you need them.

The Psalms are a terrific source of vocabulary for prayer. As a child you learned to talk by hearing others talk and imitating them; you learn to pray in the same way. For this the prayers in the Bible are invaluable. Sometimes you want to talk to God in plain English, and the words flow. But if you're like most people, there are times when your mundane prose doesn't capture the heart flood you want to convey. At those times, borrow the poetry of the Psalms.

The psalmists cut loose and whined to God:

> *I am worn out from groaning;*
> *all night long I flood my bed with weeping*
> *and drench my couch with tears.* (Psalm 6:6)

> *How long, O LORD? Will you forget me forever?*
> *How long will you hide your face from me?* (Psalm 13:1)

They gave free rein to their whining and let it propel them back to their convictions about God:

> *But I trust in your unfailing love;*
> *my heart rejoices in your salvation.* (Psalm 13:5)

The Psalms offer a startling example of how to handle intense anger without sin (Psalm 4:4). One style of psalm, the lament, includes a section in which the psalmist calls down God's wrath on those who have sinned against Israel or the psalmist personally (see Psalms 12, 35, 58, 59, 69, 70, 83, 109, 137, 140). The language pulls no punches:

> *O Daughter of Babylon, doomed to destruction,*
> *happy is he who repays you*
> *for what you have done to us —*
> *he who seizes your infants*
> *and dashes them against the rocks.* (Psalm 137:8-9)

The psalmists express this rage to God, who can handle it. Venting at God in this way will help you acknowledge angry feelings without venting them at people. You can feel anger, express anger to God, and then treat people with respect and forgiveness.

The Psalms will give you ideas for what to pray in different situations:

Help, LORD. (Psalm 12:1)

Show the wonder of your great love. . .
Keep me as the apple of your eye. (Psalm 17:7-8)

May the LORD answer you when you are in distress;
may the name of the God of Jacob protect you. . .
May he give you the desire of your heart
and make all your plans succeed. (Psalm 20:1,4)

"Show me, O LORD, my life's end
and the number of my days;
let me know how fleeting is my life." (Psalm 39:4)

Search me, O God, and know my heart;
test me and know my anxious thoughts.
See if there is any offensive way in me,
and lead me in the way everlasting. (Psalm 139:23-24)

Instead of selecting some verses and ignoring others, try to read each psalm as a unit. Each one is carefully crafted to be a balanced whole. The complaint and the praise in Psalm 13 are more powerful together and more true to genuine faith than either would be alone. The recounted memories of Psalm 44 are the springboard for the requests later in the psalm. Look for the connections between the different parts.

Images of the unimaginable.

Poetry trains your imagination. God is indescribable except in figures of speech that evoke more than they say. Envision the unimaginable God as a Rock, a Shield, a Fortress. What do these images tell you about Him?

> *He alone is my rock and my salvation;*
> *he is my fortress, I will never be shaken.* (Psalm 62:2)

Feeling nervous about a challenge you're facing? Close your eyes and picture yourself lying in a green field beside a quiet lake with God your Shepherd watching over you and restoring your soul (Psalm 23:1-2). Imagine Him satisfying your soul "as with the richest of foods" (Psalm 63:5). Pray to experience the truth of these images, and allow your body and mind to yield to the Spirit speaking through the poetry.

Training in worship.

The Psalms are Israel's book of worship music. They continue to be the church's paramount source of lyrics for prayer and praise. Your church community probably sings many songs based on the Psalms. With the psalmists as your mentors, you can learn to worship by describing God's great deeds and attributes and by thanking Him for specific things He's done in your life. The psalmists have ways of talking about God and to God that draw you into an awareness of God's presence. He becomes greater in your eyes, and the hassles of your personal life shrink.

Instructions about how life works.

Some of the Psalms belong to the Wisdom tradition. (For more on **wisdom,** see page 157.) Psalm 37, for example, uses poetry to express the smart way to live in a world where unscrupulous people seem to win. Many of the Psalms teach about God's justice, goodness, kindness, holiness, loyalty, power, compassion, and other qualities.

Insight into God the Poet.

In addition to the Psalms, much of the rest of the Old Testament is written in poetry. Try putting together two pictures in your mind: God the Lawgiver and God the Poet. What aspects of the world are best discussed in straight prose, in rational logic? What aspects require imagery and passion? What does it say about God that He pulls all these aspects together into one full view of things?

Exercise

Read some Psalms and write down everything they tell you about God. Then use those insights to worship Him.

Through the Psalms, God manages to convey some powerful ideas in imaginative language. Allow the Psalms to help you grow both in the ideas you have about the world and the creative ways in which you can think and feel about them.

*Lady Wisdom goes out
in the street and shouts.
At the town center
she makes her speech.*

Proverbs 1:20, MSG

What Can I Learn from

Proverbs and
Wisdom Books?

"Wisdom is the ability to make godly choices in life."[9] It's the ability to weigh what's important and make God-honoring choices about things as practical as borrowing money, making friends, and facing suffering. It combines street smarts with God's value system.

Wisdom is also a type of literature popular throughout the ancient world. The Proverbs are the best-known example. Wisdom literature:

- Expresses its ideas in "concise, memorable, simple, and profound" terms[10]
- Observes life as it is, sometimes with gritty realism
- Avoids falsely spiritualizing things
- Speaks with the voice of experience
- Is reflective and thoughtful
- Deals with the confusing, painful side of life
- Aims at practical skills for real life, not just abstract theory

Books of Wisdom

Proverbs
Some Psalms
Ecclesiastes
Job
Song of Songs

Wisdom is not about IQ or slick talk. People who speak slowly and choose their words carefully are often wiser than people who appear cool or witty. Still, the people who wrote the Bible's Wisdom Books had perceptive minds and a way with words.

The Wisdom Books can help you grow in wisdom—no surprise. However, you need to know a few things about how Wisdom Books work in order to avoid the two or three most common ways people misunderstand these books.

Avoid reading pieces of these books out of context.

Taking sound bites out of Wisdom Books can lead you in the opposite direction of what the writer intended. For example, Ecclesiastes 3:1-2 says,

> *There is a time for everything*
> *and a season for every activity under heaven:*
> *a time to be born and a time to die,*
> *a time to plant and a time to uproot.*

How nice that sounds! Taken on its own, it could sound like the writer means God has every up and down of your life planned and under control. Psalm 139 means that, but Ecclesiastes 3 doesn't. Ecclesiastes means something more disturbing. It goes on:

> *I also thought, "As for men, God tests them so that they may see that they are like the animals. Man's fate is like that of the animals; the same fate awaits them both: As one dies, so dies the other. . . . Everything is meaningless. All go to the same place; all come from dust, and to dust all return." (Ecclesiastes 3:18-20)*

The writer of Ecclesiastes is actually building a case for a false viewpoint that echoes Buddhism and existentialism: Life's cycles of birth and death point to the ultimate meaninglessness of this world. He's setting you up to view life through a starkly cynical lens so he can hit you with the punch line at the end of his book: Life is meaningless *unless you live it with a constant awareness of your Creator* (12:1-14). That which lies beyond this world is the only thing that can give meaning to your life in this world. That's a powerful insight, but you won't get it if you try to make sense of Ecclesiastes in bits and pieces.

Similarly, most of the book of Job consists of speeches by people who claim to be wise enough to understand God. In the end, though, God appears and dismisses all their verbiage as pretentious and offensive to Him. If you pull out bits of their speeches that sound nice, you'll end up with your thinking as warped as theirs.

Avoid treating the proverbial principles of these books as ironclad laws.

Ecclesiastes and Job are subtle and fairly intellectual books. Proverbs, on the other hand, is as down-to-earth as an Iowa farmer. Maybe that's why it's so popular. Like farm wisdom, Proverbs offers you basic values which, if you live by them, will maximize your chance of being a reasonably happy, responsible, godly adult. The proverbs have catchy ways of saying that wise people avoid violent crime, impetuous lending, wild spending, laziness, lying, and sexual promiscuity. They state things in black-and-white terms:

The plans of the diligent lead to profit
as surely as haste leads to poverty. (Proverbs 21:5)

When a man's ways are pleasing to the LORD,
he makes even his enemies live at peace with him. (Proverbs 16:7)

While the language of Proverbs is black-and-white, fools-versus-wise, always-or-never, the intent is not to give God's guaranteed promise that 100 percent of the time you'll make money if you're diligent or make peace with your enemies if you do the right thing. Proverbs are meant to teach you values, to convince you that all things being equal, diligence is the most likely path to a decent income. Pleasing God is a good investment even when you have enemies. These values are your best bet for godly, successful living, but they're not like the laws of physics. Sometimes even godly people work hard and think carefully, but lose the farm anyway. History is full of people from Martin Luther to Martin Luther King who did things that were pleasing to the Lord and got anything but peace from their enemies. Too many parents have claimed Proverbs 22:6 as a promise—"Train up a child in the way he should go, even when he is old he will not depart from it" (NASB)—and have become bitter when their children persisted in rebellion. They blame God for not coming through, or they blame themselves for doing the formula wrong. But proverbs aren't formulas. They are wise values.

Use God's definition of success.

Many of the proverbs discuss making money, gaining people's approval, and having life work out to your liking. If you select these in isolation, they sound like God's formula for a successful, self-centered life. But the refrain that runs through the Wisdom Books is, "the fear of the LORD is the beginning of wisdom" (Psalm 111:10). Taken as a whole, the Wisdom Books make it clear that God is not all that interested in making your self-centered life work out. God is interested in growing you into a human being who fears Him (takes Him seriously) and values the things He values. Sometimes this agenda requires upsetting your agenda drastically. The wisdom writers never tire of pointing out this annoying fact.

Don't over-spiritualize when wisdom says startling things about sex.

Historically, a lot of people have been uncomfortable with a book like the Song of Songs in the Bible. It describes romantic, sexual love in the vivid imagery of passionate love poetry. Many centuries after it was written, a rabbi suggested that it must be about the love between God and His people, and Christians uneasy with human romance jumped on that idea. However, few serious scholars today question that the book was intended to be an abandoned celebration of romance between a committed, monogamous human couple.

Today, when sex is often treated like a bodily function that people just need to "get" on a regular basis with whomever, Song of Songs provides valuable wisdom.

Many people who have had instant gratification of their sexual desires since adolescence, with multiple partners, report burnout of their ability to feel romantic passion. Many television programs and pop songs strip romance of its poetry, mystery, and beauty—its capacity to draw two people into a transcendent unity that can survive decades of commitment. If you're cynical about the joys of monogamy, the Song of Songs can heal the numb parts of your soul. Instead of describing sex as a biology lesson or game of conquest, it uses images to coax a soul into life:

> Let him kiss me with the kisses of his mouth—
> for your love is more delightful than wine.
> Pleasing is the fragrance of your perfumes;
> your name is like perfume poured out.
>
> Your two breasts are like two fawns,
> like twin fawns of a gazelle
> that browse among the lilies.
> Until the day breaks
> and the shadows flee,
> I will go to the mountain of myrrh
> and to the hill of incense.
>
> Place me like a seal over your heart,
> like a seal on your arm;
> for love is as strong as death,
> its jealousy unyielding as the grave. . .
> Many waters cannot quench love;
> rivers cannot wash it away.
> If one were to give
> all the wealth of his house for love,
> it would be utterly scorned.
> (Song of Songs 1:2-3; 4:5-6; 8:6-7)

It's true that marital love is a symbol and foretaste of the love between Christ and His people (Ephesians 5:25-33), but marriage should never be spiritualized to mean only that. In fact, marriage is a powerful symbol precisely because monogamous passion is so powerful in itself—"as strong as death."

There are lots of biblical books that can teach you about God's love for you. Let the Song of Songs teach you about something less important than that, but still vital to your life as a whole human person: the possibilities of ecstasy in marriage when two people have souls alive to the beauty of human love. What does it say about God that He invented that?

What Can I Learn from the Prophets?

> *That's why I use prophets
> to shake you to attention,
> why my words
> cut you to the quick:
> To wake you to my judgment
> blazing like light.
> I'm after love that lasts,
> not more religion.*
>
> **Hosea 6:5-6, MSG**

Many people assume that prophecy is mainly about foretelling the future. That's what the word means in pagan (Greek and Roman) and occult settings. But the Hebrew prophets were more *forthtellers* about the present than *foretellers* of the future. Their main job was to speak for God to their contemporaries. "Of the hundreds of prophets in ancient Israel in Old Testament times, only sixteen were chosen to speak oracles (messages from God) that would be collected and written up into books."[11] The books of Old Testament history have much to say about the prophets who didn't write books. Those prophets spoke to their contemporaries about things people were doing at that time. The sixteen prophets who wrote

Books of the Prophets

Isaiah
Jeremiah
Ezekiel
Hosea
Joel
Amos
Obadiah
Jonah
Micah
Nahum
Habakkuk
Zephaniah
Haggai
Zechariah
Malachi

down their prophecies in biblical books also spent most of their time addressing the situations of their day.

> Less than 2 percent of Old Testament prophecy is messianic [about Christ]. Less than 5 percent specifically describes the New Covenant age. Less than 1 percent concerns events yet to come.[12]

Therefore, if your main interest in the Prophets is predictions about the future, you may be disappointed. The Prophets interweave present-telling, near-future-telling and far-future-telling, so you'll have trouble isolating just the cool end-times passages you're looking for. For example, notice how Micah 5:1-5 mingles predictions about Christ's birth with insights into the end of this age. Also, because the prophets wrote in poetry and symbols, there's plenty of room for disagreement on how to interpret the prophecies about events that haven't happened yet.

Predictions about the Messiah and New Covenant times.

Still, the handful of prophecies that do point to Christ and the New Covenant are well worth knowing. They will help you understand who Christ is and what He came to earth to do. The New Testament writers had these prophecies in their minds when they wrote about Christ. These prophecies also underscore the fact that sending Christ was not an idea God thought up late in the game, but was part of His unfolding plan from the beginning.

A few of these passages are:
- Isaiah 9:1-7
- Isaiah 11:1-9
- Isaiah 49:1-7
- Isaiah 52:13–53:12
- Isaiah 61:1-11
- Jeremiah 31:31-34

- Ezekiel 36:22-32
- Joel 2:28-32
- Micah 5:1-5
- Zechariah 9:9-13

Nine Miraculous Changes

The prophets predicted nine areas in which the world would change miraculously when the Messiah came:[13]

1. Improvements in the climate and natural elements (Isaiah 30:23-26; Ezekiel 47:1-12; Joel 2:21-26; Zechariah 14:8)
2. Unprecedented growth and fruitage of trees (Isaiah 41:17-20; Ezekiel 36:8-11,29-30; 47:6-7,12; Joel 2:21-26)
3. Productivity of animals, including fish (Jeremiah 31:10-12; Ezekiel 36:11; 47:8-10)
4. A superabundance of food (Psalm 72:16; Isaiah 30:23-24; Jeremiah 31:10-14; Ezekiel 34:25-30; 36:29-30; Joel 2:21-26; Zechariah 8:11-12)
5. An abundance of wine (Jeremiah 31:10-12; Joel 2:21-26; Amos 9:13; Zechariah 8:11-12)
6. Peace among animals (Isaiah 11:6-9; 65:23-25)
7. Protection from ordinary hazards (Isaiah 11:8-9; 65:23-25; Ezekiel 34:25-29)
8. Physical healing (Isaiah 29:18; 33:24; 35:5-6)
9. Longevity of life (Isaiah 65:20-22)

Predictions about events that are yet to come.

If you can avoid getting so obsessed with these predictions that you give too little attention to other issues in the Bible, end-times prophecies can help you put your life into perspective. The world is not going to be a sewer of injustice and suffering forever. Nor is the futile cycle of birth and death described in Ecclesiastes the whole story. History is going somewhere, and if your allegiance is with God, it's going somewhere good for you.

It's hard to isolate the prophecies about the very last things from those that deal with nearer-future events because God wove them together. The first coming of Christ was the beginning-of-the-end, and the second coming will be the end-of-the-end. We have been in the "end times" for two thousand years, and the prophets saw it all as one big mural of many overlapping images.

Here are some of the passages that contain end-times predictions:

- Isaiah 35
- Isaiah 65:17–66:24
- Ezekiel 38–48
- Daniel 7–12
- Joel 3
- Amos 9:11-15
- Micah 4:1-5
- Zechariah 9:14-17

God's passion for justice and covenant loyalty.

If you really want to learn to see the world from God's perspective, here is an area where the Prophets can help you. Their main job was to state how well Israel was keeping the nation's end of the covenant. They compared the Law with the people's actual behavior and declared both God's verdict and the consequences Israel could expect. The Law had explained the consequences beforehand, so the Prophets merely announced the enforcement of the agreement already in place. (For more on **seeing the world from God's perspective,** see page 22. For more on **the covenant,** see page 144.)

Because the prophets carried out their task with such colorful language, you can see God going through the full range of emotions as He acts as a passionately loving yet firm Parent. He's furious at betrayal; He's cut to the heart; His compassion is so intense that He can hardly stand to give His children the discipline they deserve and need. He wants them to grow up into responsible adults, so He can't keep bailing them out forever. He warns and warns, but finally He withdraws His protection and allows them to suffer the awful consequences of their hardheartedness. This whole drama gets played out in the books of the Prophets.

You can learn a lot about God as Parent from the Prophets. But because these books are about God parenting incredibly rebellious teenagers, the picture isn't pretty. You may even recoil, especially if your own parents weren't models of justice and mercy. So if you find yourself put off by God's anger, look at what God is angry *about*:

- The rich and powerful exploiting the poor and vulnerable
- Dirty legal maneuvering
- Lack of compassion toward needy people
- Environmental degradation
- Worship of other gods who promise money and power
- Corrupt political leaders
- Murder
- Outward shows of religious piety to conceal widespread indifference to ethical living

The Prophets can be hard to read because they discuss current events with unfamiliar names of people and places—it's like picking up the newspaper in a foreign country. Even worse, they do it with poetry. However, if you use a commentary to get over these challenges, you'll find the themes the Prophets address are as relevant as this morning's news.

Exercise

Read one of the books of the Prophets, such as Amos. Underline everything said about the use of money. Look for references to the rich, the needy, silver, gold, injustice, righteousness, and so on. Why do you think God cares so much about how His people use money? How does this affect your view of money in your personal life and nationally?

God's majestic rule over all of time and space.

The Law is addressed to a single nation: Israel. But the Prophets declare God's justice for all nations and the whole universe. Isaiah 13–23, for example, is a series of formal statements in which God condemns the evil behavior of each of the nations surrounding Israel. Even though they don't recognize God as their King, He still claims the right to judge them. Isaiah 26 discusses the devastation of the entire planet because of human indifference to the covenant that came before Israel's Law—the covenant God made with all humanity to care for the earth (Genesis 9:1-17). Isaiah 65:17–66:24 promises a new heaven and a new earth.

The very language of the Prophets will enfold you in God's majesty. If you have a cramped, limited view of God, the Prophets will explode it. Their God is huge.

What Can I
Learn from
the Gospels?

"Are you tired? Worn out? Burned out on religion? Come to me. Get away with me and you'll recover your life. . . . Walk with me and work with me — watch how I do it. Learn the unforced rhythms of grace. . . . Keep company with me and you'll learn to live freely and lightly."

Matthew 11:28-30, MSG

An experience of Jesus the Messiah.

The Bible as a whole is about God. The Gospels are about God the Son — Jesus Christ. The entire Old Testament story builds up to the revelation of God in Christ.

In Jesus you see "the heart-wrenching goodness of God, his incomprehensible graciousness and generosity." The chief purpose of reading and rereading the Gospels, then, is to experience Jesus, "to hold him before the mind with as much fullness and clarity as possible" so you can see how He lived with "beauty, truth, and power."[14]

Jesus' original disciples had a tremendous opportunity: They followed Him around for more than three years, watching what He did, hearing what He said, and trying to imitate Him. You have an equally tremendous opportunity. If you cooperate with the Holy Spirit, He will bring the stories and teachings of Jesus alive for you so that you can watch and hear and imitate Him too. (For more on **Jesus,** see page 30. For more on **Jesus' wisdom in the Gospels,** see page 19.)

Many people read the Gospels to learn about themselves. It's good to understand yourself, but don't let that be the focus of your Gospel reading. If you want to experience Jesus, focus on Jesus: who He is, what He does, how He says you should live. Notice the difference between two different approaches to the same gospel story.

Two Views of Luke 8:40-56

In this passage Jesus agrees to heal a child, then a woman's need sidetracks Him, then the child dies during the delay and He raises the child from death.

Me-centered view: How am I like the bleeding woman in this story? What healing do I need? What am I ashamed of? How have I been excluded from the community? In what areas am I afraid to reach out to touch Jesus? How can I have the faith this woman has? How can I be like Jesus and offer others a healing touch?

Jesus-centered view: What does Jesus say and do in this story? How does He treat the father? The woman? The child? The other people? What is important to Him here? How does He show Himself to be the King with full authority in the world? What response from people does He seek? Is this a King I would be glad to follow? What will my life be like if this is the King I follow? How will I feel, think, talk, and act if I truly see Jesus in this way? What is Jesus saying to me through this story? Holy Spirit, please enable me to see and respond to Jesus the way the woman and father in this story do.

The "me-centered" questions in the box above aren't bad. There are times for asking them. But you'll find that if you focus on Jesus, you'll be naturally drawn to respond with the faith of the bleeding woman—Jesus just has that effect. However, if you focus on yourself and your faith—or lack of it—you'll understand your problems better but make less progress toward letting Jesus solve them. So you needn't forbid yourself from asking any "me" questions at all, but be aware of where your focus lies.

Also, imagine yourself in the place of the disciples. Put yourself in the scene, watching Jesus heal, hearing Him teach. Identify with their confusion or discovery. What would you have thought and felt in their place? What picture of Him is forming in your mind? What is your life like if the Messiah is like this? Jesus often goes away alone to pray — is that something a disciple should imitate? Even if you've been a Christian for a long time and have experience leading or discipling others, it's a good idea to put yourself in the place of one who is still learning at the feet of Jesus. He is, after all, the premier spiritual teacher in all of history.

There are at least three ways of approaching the Gospels, and many methods under each approach:

> ## You and the Disciples
>
> • What do the disciples understand about Jesus and His teaching?
> • What don't they understand?
> • What practical assignments does Jesus give them?
> • How do they do?
> • How can you learn from their successes and mistakes?

- **Study.** It's valuable to study the Gospels so you understand accurately what Jesus meant by something like, "Blessed are you who are poor, for yours is the kingdom of God" (Luke 6:20). (For more on **study,** see pages 79-109.)
- **Read in context.** If you pay attention to little phrases like "that day" (Mark 4:35), you can see that Mark 4–6 is meant to lay out events of a single day. It's a good idea to read that whole section as a connected unit. Jesus moves from teaching about the kingdom to doing the works of the kingdom. He teaches with authority, then acts with authority. Try to take in the whole movie as well as analyze individual scenes — the whole will help you make sense of the scenes. Get the big picture of what Jesus does; notice the phrases and ideas He keeps repeating.
- **Meditate.** Beyond understanding the Gospels is experiencing the Jesus of the Gospels. Immerse yourself in one scene or one bit of teaching until it becomes part of you. (For more on **meditation,** see page 71.)

An experience of the kingdom of God.

The Gospel writers' chief goal was to show that Jesus was the Messiah, the King foretold by the Prophets. Each of His miracles pointed back to prophecies about what people should expect when the King ushered in what the Gospels call "the kingdom of heaven" (Matthew) or "the kingdom of God" (Mark, Luke, John). (For more on **the kingdom,** see page 32.) If you read one of the Gospels and circle every instance of the word *kingdom*, you'll find it is the core of Jesus' teaching. But what is the kingdom?

The kingdom includes all parts of all universes in which what God wants done is done. In our universe (we know nothing about others), the stars and planets obey God's laws of physics. The angels also do what God wants done. However, God made humans His deputy governors of earth but they rebelled (Genesis 1–3). God allowed them to create social and political institutions and private lives that lay outside His kingdom. Human rebellion actually altered earth's climate, ecosystems, human lifespan, physical health, mental health, social relations, and relationship with God. So God launched His plan to mend the damage. Through the Prophets, He promised to restore the planet and human life to their ideal conditions when the King came to spread His reign throughout the earth. That was and is Jesus' mission, and that's why healings, authority over weather, and even ability to make wine from water are important signs in the Gospels.

The kingdom is already-but-not-yet. Ever since Christ came to earth, the kingdom has been in our midst. You can live in the kingdom now. But until Christ returns a second time to bring the kingdom in its fullness, its presence will be partial for everyone and invisible to many.

You can believe in theory that Jesus is the Son of God, but the rubber meets the road when you decide each day to follow Him as King. The Gospels will help you come to grips with questions like:

- What exactly is the kingdom?
- How is the kingdom already at work around me?
- How do things work in the kingdom differently from the way I'm used to things working?

- What's important in the kingdom? What's not important?
- How is my life affected if Jesus has royal authority over planets, weather, disease, food, and everything else?
- How do I experience the kingdom and live as an active part of it?

Right now, in your midst, Jesus is at work spreading His kingdom. It's smack in front of you, and you'll see it if you put on gospel glasses.

> ### Exercise
>
> In the world, loving your enemies is pointless. In the kingdom, loving your enemies is the normal way of life (Matthew 5:43-48). Why the difference?

An experience of Christ's death and resurrection.

You can have correct doctrine about the Cross, but that alone won't help you much. What you really need is to be so gripped by the fact that Jesus gave His life on the cross for you that you are motivated to love and adore Him. Meditating on the gospel accounts of Jesus' trial and execution can penetrate your heart with this event. It really happened. Let it dominate your thinking more than whatever happened to you ten years ago or last Thursday.

Likewise, correct doctrine about the resurrection is good, but having it vividly in your mind as an actual historical event is better. Meditating on the resurrection accounts in the Gospels will help you love and adore the God who was able to raise Jesus from the dead, the God who triumphed over sin and death through the resurrection, the Jesus who proved Himself to be King by rising from the dead. Immerse yourself in this event until you see the world through the fact that Jesus is master of the created universe and of history.

What Can I
Learn from the
Book of Acts?

A picture of your life-purpose as part of God's kingdom.

The same author wrote the Gospel of Luke and the book of Acts. They are a two-volume work that explains how Jesus, the Jewish Messiah, established a kingdom open to people of all ethnic groups who put their faith in His death for their sin. The Gospel covers the life of Jesus, with special emphasis on His years of ministry, death, and resurrection. Acts picks up the story just after the resurrection and tells how God's people spread the ministry of Jesus to key cities throughout the Roman Empire in about thirty years.

In both volumes, "the identifying mark of those who have entered this kingdom is the indwelling, empowering presence of the Holy Spirit, not the traditional identity marks of Judaism (circumcision and Law observance)."[15]

Exercise

Look for all the references to the Holy Spirit in Acts. What do you learn about what the Spirit's like and how He operates?

So Luke-Acts is about how King Jesus established and spread His kingdom of the New Covenant. (For more on the **New Covenant,** see page 148.)

Acts doesn't have much to say about your private, individual relationship with God. Instead, it portrays teams of people, empowered by the Holy Spirit, building kingdom outposts—New Covenant communities. In Acts, individuals make contributions that continue to echo through the centuries because these people focus on the Spirit's global agenda.

Old Testament stories can be read on three levels:
- God's plan to rescue the whole world
- Israel's role in that plan, and how the nation did or didn't cooperate
- The role of individuals in contributing to the plan

(For more on **Old Testament stories,** see page 138.)

The same three levels apply to Luke-Acts:
- The top level is God's plan to rescue the whole world through Jesus Christ.
- The second level is the church's (the community of believers) role in that plan, worked out under King Jesus through the power of the Spirit.
- The bottom level is how individuals like Stephen, Paul, Priscilla, and even humble Dorcas contributed to the church's role in the plan.

It's easy to read Acts and focus on the human stars, such as Peter and Paul. But as with the rest of the Bible, God is always the Hero of the story. And even if your role in the plan is not to be a star like Paul, there are plenty of other roles that are vital to the drama. The important thing is to focus not on yourself ("What is my role in the drama? Is it important enough? Can I do it?") but on God and His plan ("What is God doing in history and today? What does God want done? Where is the Holy Spirit already at work and inviting me to pitch in?").

Exercise

If you're used to thinking of yourself as flying solo, read both Acts and the Epistles for God's habit of accomplishing His purposes through teams.

A picture of how the kingdom works in the nitty-gritty of real church communities.

The believers of Acts are committed to King Jesus and filled with the Holy Spirit. But they have flaws—plenty of them. Even apostles debate what the Spirit is saying to them. If you have an idealized picture of what a church should be like, Acts will give you a realistic picture of what a church can be like and still contribute to God's plan.

In some cases, practical models of how God's people should go about things.

When you read in the Bible an account of something somebody did, you'll often find yourself asking, "Is this story simply recording *what they did then*, or is it offering a model of *what I or the church should do today?*" Acts seems to raise that question frequently. For example, is Acts 6:1-6 the standard for choosing "deacons" in a local church to assist the "apostles" in caring for needy church members? Is 13:1-3 the standard way to choose missionaries? Should prophets be functioning in churches today the way they function in Acts? Is this or that story a pattern or a unique situation?

Here are some criteria to think about:

- **Is this behavior a recurring theme in Acts?** If it's mentioned once, it might be a unique case. If Luke took the trouble to mention it over and over, he might have intended it to be a pattern.

- **Does the behavior relate to Luke's chief themes?** These include: God's eternal purpose to save people through Jesus Christ; the universal availability of salvation without the requirement to keep the Jewish Law; God's people participating in God's plan by the power of the Spirit, despite suffering; and so on. The closer a behavior in Acts is to one of Luke's themes, the more likely it is to be a model.

- **What's the function of this behavior? Is it a core function of the church?** Be aware of the difference between form and function. Eating is a function. McDonald's, a home-cooked banquet, and frozen dinners are three forms this function could take. Shelter is a function. Igloos, teepees, thatched-roof cottages, and condos are some forms of shelter. Passing the teachings of Jesus to new believers is a function. Preaching, group Bible study, private Bible reading, meditation, and audiotapes are some of the forms in which the teachings of Jesus can be passed on. Sometimes the functions described in Acts are meant to be patterns for all generations to follow (for example, it's important to care for impoverished believers in some way), while the forms can be flexible from generation to generation.

- **Do the Gospels or Epistles talk about this?** If another part of the New Testament gives explicit instruction in this area, then it's probably a model to follow.

What Can I Learn from

We saw it, we heard it, and now we're telling you so you can experience it along with us, this experience of communion with the Father and his Son, Jesus Christ.

1 John 1:3, MSG

the Epistles?

Epistle is an old word for letter, the kind you mail. The New Testament Epistles are simply letters mailed from an apostle or elder of the earliest community of Christ's followers. Most of them were addressed to communities based in various cities throughout the Roman Empire. A few were addressed to individuals. (The title of each letter identifies the recipients: Colossians is the letter to believers in the city of Colossae, and so on.) The letters were read aloud for the benefit of the whole community, and the recipients saved them to share with neighboring communities.

When you read these letters, think of them as one side of an e-mail conversation. A specific situation prompted someone to write each letter,

Epistles

Romans
1 & 2 Corinthians
Galatians
Ephesians
Philippians
Colossians
1 & 2 Thessalonians
1 & 2 Timothy
Titus
Philemon
Hebrews
James
1 & 2 Peter
1, 2, & 3 John
Jude

even though the letter was going to be reread by others outside that situation. The writer assumed his readers knew all about the situation, remembered things he had said and done while visiting them, and even knew what they had written in previous letters. Scholars have worked hard to piece together as much of this background as possible; you'll find the letters make much more sense if you obtain some of this basic information. (For more on **background,** see pages 93-109.)

The letters are the most logical of the biblical books. While other books convey God's message through story and poetry, the letters use step-by-step reasoning. Hence, to get the writer's point, you need to follow the reasoning. To do this:

- **Think from the top down.** It's best to read the whole letter first to get the big picture. What topics are addressed in turn? What do you learn about the first readers of this letter?

- **Make an outline** or find one in your study Bible. Two typical outlines for Paul are:

  I. *Greeting*

  II. *Thanksgiving*

  III. *Body of Letter:* What God has done through Christ and is continuing to do through the Spirit

  IV. *Moral Exhortation:* How you should live in light of what God has done and is doing

  V. *Closing*

  I. *Greeting*

  II. *Thanksgiving*

  III. *Body* (addresses problem #1, problem #2, problem #3)

  IV. *Closing*

- **Think paragraphs.** Within each main section of the letter, what's the big idea of each paragraph? How is each paragraph connected to the one before and the one after so that there's a train of thought?

(For more on **paragraphs and context,** see page 85.)

A grateful awareness of what God has done for you through Christ.

The point of reading the letters is not to equip you to win doctrinal arguments. The point is for you to become gripped by what God has done for you and then to respond. You'll need to understand what the writer is saying so that you won't become gripped by something that isn't true. Still, this is more than just an intellectual exercise. What are the incredible truths that led this letter writer to go to unbelievable lengths to proclaim them? Paul, for example, walked several thousand miles on stone roads and across mountains, in the rain and sometimes without dinner, occasionally enduring beatings and being jailed, in order to get people this information. His colleagues hand-carried these letters, often hundreds of miles, to their destinations. What was so vital that Paul had to say? As you read the letters, put yourself into the frame of mind that expects to be knocked over by what you read. Christ died for you—so what?

- Do you really believe that without Christ you would be "dead in sin," living a meaningless existence, and your destiny would be worse than nothingness? Exactly how bad is being "dead in sin"?
- Do you really believe it cost the Father and Christ a huge price to rescue you from that mess? Exactly what did it cost them?
- Do you really believe that Christ has won for you. . .
  meaning
  eternal joy
  a chance to be intimate with the most glorious Being imaginable
  an important role in God's plan
  and more?

The letters can make all that vividly real for you.

These days, a lot of people are concerned about having an "identity," about finding out "who they are" and "making a statement" about who they are. The letters will tell you who you are and how to make a statement about it.

An awareness that the risen Jesus is with you here and now.

For Paul, Peter, John, and the rest, Jesus' presence was a constant experience. Not only did they explain that this was so in their letters, you can feel it in their excitement about life, in their attitude toward prison and persecution, in their response to questions from their readers. This awareness is contagious if you read with your mind open to it.

An awareness of Jesus' and the Holy Spirit's current activity in the community of God's people.

The letters were written for and/or about communities of people who were struggling to follow the King together. The problems the letters address would never have arisen had not God been trying to forge

> . . . a chosen people, a royal priesthood, a holy nation, a people belonging to God, that you [plural] may declare the praises of him who called you out of darkness into his wonderful light. (1 Peter 2:9)

> Consequently, you are no longer foreigners and aliens, but fellow citizens with God's people and members of God's household, built on the foundation of the apostles and prophets, with Christ Jesus himself as the chief cornerstone. In him the whole building is joined together and rises to become a holy temple in the Lord. And in him you too are being built together to become a dwelling in which God lives by his Spirit. (Ephesians 2:19-21)

Questions for the Letters

• What were the Holy Spirit's priorities in that church?

• How did He want people to look at things?

• What did He want people to do?

• What light does this shed on His priorities for my community? On how He wants us and me to see things? On what He wants me to do?

• Who am I in Christ?

• How does a person in Christ act?

For example, the problems in 1 Corinthians include factions in the church community (1:10-4:21), how one member's sin affects the whole community (5:1-13), lawsuits among community members (6:1-11), whether members of the community should marry (7:1-40), how some members' convictions about food restrictions affect others in the group (8:1–11:1), community worship (11:2-34), spiritual gifts for building up the community (12:1-31), and so on. Little of this would be significant if believers were supposed to cultivate their individual relationships with God as hermits. But the Holy Spirit's agenda is to build a temple for God out of humans in relationship with each other as well as with God. The letters give you snapshots of the Spirit at work on this project in several different cities. These snapshots will help you notice and participate in this work in a local group of believers in your own town, as well as in the international community of all God's people. (For more on **the church,** see page 35.)

The most common word the New Testament letter writers use for the community is "church." This word has nothing to do with buildings and everything to do with people in relationship. A "church" can meet in a home, a restaurant, or a fabulous edifice as long as the people are doing the things described in the letters. The letters will tell you what God means by "church" and your place in the "church."

> So the continuing incarnation of the divine Son in his gathered people must fill our minds if we are to love him and his Father adequately and thus live on the rock of hearing and doing.[16]

A picture of how you will lead your life if you are truly grateful for Christ's work and truly aware of His ongoing presence.

The letters are full of instructions on how to live. Almost all of this is impossible—and maybe not even sensible—to do if you aren't deeply convinced of what Christ has done and if you're not in partnership with the Holy Spirit.

> *Therefore, as God's chosen people, holy and dearly loved, clothe yourselves with compassion, kindness, humility, gentleness and patience. Bear with each other and forgive whatever grievances you may have against one another. Forgive as the Lord forgave you.* (Colossians 3:12-13)

Clothing yourself with compassion and patience is not easy, especially for some personalities. Partnership with the Spirit is essential here. Christlike forgiveness doesn't even make sense unless you're convinced of your identity: you're part of God's chosen people, dearly loved, set apart for a purpose, and forgiven for more than you could ever have to forgive someone else. The test of whether you really believe this stuff is whether you are living this way.

What Can I Learn from
Revelation?

Encouragement that no matter what's happening to you now, the end of the story is secure.

The chief purpose of Revelation is encouragement. God's people in western Turkey were suffering for their faith and fearful that it was all for nothing. The writer John was overseeing those churches, and God gave him a glimpse of the end game so John could encourage the people with his visions. In Revelation, God assures you that:

- God's kingdom is unstoppable.
- Nevertheless, God's enemies will not cease trying to stop it until God decides it's time to wrap up the struggle.
- In the meantime, God has good reasons for allowing His people to suffer terrible afflictions.
- Things will get worse before they get better.

- However, when they get better, they'll be so great that you'll agree it was all worth it.
- No unjust person will "get away with it," and no act of courage will go unrewarded.

Don't be intimidated by the symbolic language in Revelation. This book was written in a style familiar in John's day, the style of *apocalyptic literature*. (The word *revelation* is a translation of the Greek word *apocalypse*.) This style was familiar in John's day among suffering peoples of the Middle East. Apocalyptic literature used well-known symbols (such as the sea, which usually represented the forces of chaos arrayed against God) to create vivid images of the final defeat of evildoers by God. A good commentary can help you understand the symbols that were standard in those days. A commentary can also help you with symbols that are unique to Revelation, although it's harder to be precise about those.

Still, even if you can't be sure about every symbol and a precise timetable of when it will all happen, you can understand enough to get John's point: Jesus wins in the end, so keep moving ahead in faith and don't give up. Life is not an endless, meaningless cycle of birth and death; it's going somewhere, so you are too. The first time you read Revelation, you may want to just let the images wash over you to give you the big picture. (For more on **what is yet to come,** see page 36.)

The End of the Story

"At the risk of taking away the drama of life, God has told us the end of the story of history! Of course, this includes the end of our own individual stories. . . . We know roughly how the world as we know it will end:

- what will happen to the currently powerful kingdoms of the world at the end
- what will happen to the armies that opposed God

- what will happen to all people, be they great or small, at the end of the world
- what will happen to those who love God and believe in His Son, Jesus Christ
- what will happen to those who have rejected Jesus and die separated from God

"We even know what will happen to us because of the deeds we have done in faith:

- how we who have believed in Jesus will be spending much of eternity
- how those who have rejected Jesus Christ will be spending their eternity
- what will happen with all the time, money, and energy we have invested in the advancement of God's kingdom
- what will happen to all the wealth, fame, and power people have falsely gained
- what will happen to Satan and his demonic followers
- and many other fascinating things beyond these." [17]

A vision of the resurrected Jesus as a King worth worshiping.

If you have a Sunday school image of Jesus as mousy and passive, Revelation will help you forget it. The risen Christ appears to John in chapter 1, and John faints. Jesus declares,

> "Do not be afraid. I am the First and the Last. I am the Living One; I was dead, and behold I am alive for ever and ever! And I hold the keys of death and Hades. Write, therefore, what you have seen." (Revelation 1:17-19)

Jesus proceeds to give instructions for all the churches John is overseeing. He then reveals the throne room of heaven, a place of awe-inspiring worship. If you allow yourself to picture these scenes, your private world will shrink and you'll see why this is a King worth following, even into the mouth of hell.

Revelation is not primarily about Satan or the Antichrist. It's about Jesus Christ, King of a glorious kingdom in which you are invited, even now, to participate.

"Wisdom . . . isn't satisfied

with information retrieval: You can't access

wisdom by the megabyte."

Edmund P. Clowney[1]

How Can I
Read Through the Bible?

Reading through the Bible in a year hasn't worked for me. Can you suggest a plan for hitting the highlights in a year or two?

Your method of Bible reading is succeeding if it's hitting this goal: *To enable you to see the world increasingly from God's perspective.* If your Bible reading isn't helping you to think and act the way Jesus would if He were you, then you may want to consider trying different approaches.

Reading straight through the Bible works well if you already have some Bible background, if you're naturally a big reader, or if you have a friend whom you can ask questions about what you're reading. However, if this method isn't succeeding for you, there are many others you can try.

One is meditating on brief passages. This method is especially valuable if you have substantial Bible knowledge already but you're having trouble living by what you know. It's also valuable if you're currently under a lot of stress. (For more on **meditation,** see page 71.)

Here is one other method you might find helpful. For each category of books (Gospels, law, history), you'll benefit from reading up on that topic in the section that follows. You may also want to review the section, "What's the Bible about?"

For some people, reading for twenty minutes a day consistently is the most effective approach. Others benefit more from a two-hour block of time per week. Mark your calendar with a schedule that will allow you to spend two to two-and-a-half hours in the Bible each week.

Before you begin reading, pause to pray. Ask the Holy Spirit to open your mind to His voice and clear away the thoughts that distract you.

Gospels.

First read the four Gospels. Ideally, read for an hour or more at a time so you can take in the flow of the story. As you read, look for answers to these two questions:

- What does this tell me about Jesus?
- What does this tell me about the kingdom of God or kingdom of heaven?

Write down what you observe—your honest take. Try to see, hear, and smell the scenes freshly. For example, you're reading about Jesus' encounter with a paralyzed man (Matthew 9:1-8). What can you say about someone who claims the right to forgive sins? Was He a nut? What evidence do the Gospels give that Jesus may have been a nut? What evidence can you find that He wasn't a nut? What do you make of His no-holds-barred confrontations with some people and His incredible gentleness with others? How did people react to Him? Do you see anybody who mildly approved of His wise moral teaching, or did most people have stronger reactions? What does this say about Him?

If you have questions about what you read, make a list of them. Find a source that can help you: a person, a Bible dictionary, or other source whose accurate knowledge you can rely on.

When you've finished the Gospels, take a few days off from reading to reflect on what you've learned. What picture of Jesus and His kingdom is emerging? What might the Holy Spirit be saying to you?

Genesis.

Read through Genesis, looking for the top level of the story: God's plan. (For more on **God's plan,** see pages 27 and 137.) In Genesis, God created humans, was rejected by them, and then set in motion a plan to redeem all humankind through one family. Don't focus on lessons you can learn from the life of this or that human character in the story. Focus on God:

- What is God like?

So what that God created the earth? So what that He called Abraham? So what that He put Abraham through decades of painful training? What does all this tell you about God?

Acts.

Read Acts for the top level of the story: God's plan. Acts was written by the same person who wrote the Gospel of Luke, so it's like volume 2 of that Gospel. As you read, ask:

- How does the Holy Spirit continue working out God's plan in the first decades of the church?

Watch for the Holy Spirit—His methods and goals, how people interact with Him.

By now you've looked closely at Jesus, the Father, and the Spirit. You've seen how they've all pursued a single plan for the world. Take a few days off from reading to reflect. Where does your life intersect with this plan? How have you participated in the kingdom? In the church's mission? Does God interact with you personally in the way He interacted personally with the people in Genesis, the Gospels, and Acts? What is your life like if the Father, the Son, and the Spirit are all they're portrayed to be in these books? Pray about what you're discovering.

Exodus 1-19.

This section of Exodus gives important background to the New Testament drama. It will help you understand what Jesus accomplished on the cross. When you get to Paul's letters and he talks about freedom from slavery to sin, you'll benefit from having Exodus in the back of your mind. As you read, ask:

• What does this tell me about God?

What do you observe about God's goodness? God's power? God's capacity for anger and kindness? What do you make of a God who can be so fierce and yet so tender? The God of Exodus is scary. How does this picture make sense side by side with the God of the Gospels? What is your life like if this God is actively engaged in it?

Paul's letters, part 1.

You met Paul in Acts. Now you're going to read his correspondence with some churches he founded. Paul was a very logical, deep thinker. In the Bible, his letters are arranged from longest to shortest. Romans is first, but Paul's thinking there is so deep that you may want to get used to his style with some of the shorter letters. You could follow this order:

• Philippians
• Ephesians
• Colossians
• Philemon (one of the Colossians)
• Galatians

Try to follow the thread of Paul's thought from paragraph to paragraph. You won't get everything the first time, but see if you can finish a chapter and be able to explain basically what that chapter is about. Write down what Paul says about the following:

• What has God done for me in Christ?
• How should I live in light of what God has done for me?
• What problems in these churches did Paul address?

When you encounter key words, such as *redemption*, look them up in a Bible dictionary. As you begin each book, you'll benefit greatly if you read some basic background about the people to whom Paul was writing and what his main concerns were. Many study Bibles provide this information. (For more on **resources,** see pages 97-109.)

When you've read these letters, take a day off to reflect. What are the one or two things the Holy Spirit impressed on your heart from your reading of Paul? What ideas were repeated over and over? What is your life like if Paul's view of the world is true? Ask God to help you believe in your gut that this is the truth about your life.

A taste of the Law.

After reading Paul, you've heard a lot about the Law. You don't need to read the whole Law at this point, but you'll understand Paul better if you have some familiarity with the Law. For this purpose, read the following:

- Exodus 20–27; 30; 32–34; 40
- Leviticus 4–5; 16; 19

As you read, write down your observations about the following:
- What does this tell me about God and His priorities?
- What does this tell me about the meaning of Christ's death on the cross?
- What, if anything, surprises me about the Law?

Paul's letters, part 2.

Now that you've read some of the Law, you're prepared to understand why Paul says (1) the Law is good and holy, and (2) the New Covenant of Christ is better. Read the rest of Paul's letters:

- 1 & 2 Corinthians
- Romans
- 1 & 2 Thessalonians
- 1 & 2 Timothy
- Titus

As you read, ask:

- What has God done for me in Christ?
- How should I live in light of what God has done for me?
- What echoes of the Old Covenant do I see? What differences do I see?
- What are some of the issues the earliest churches struggled with?

Again, take a few days off from reading to reflect. What is the Holy Spirit saying to you? Identify a couple of passages from Paul's letters that you'll return to later for deeper meditation.

Psalms.

You've been reading books that are heavy on thinking. Now it's time to let the passionate, poetic side of the Bible balance your thinking. The Psalms will train you in prayer and worship. Take a month to read the Psalms. Write down:

- What do the psalmists say to and about God when they're angry?
- What do the psalmists say to and about God when they're sad?
- What do the psalmists say to and about God when they're afraid?
- What do the psalmists say to and about God when they're grateful?
- What do the psalmists say to and about God when they're joyful?

Pause to check in with yourself. You've covered a lot of material, from the Gospels to the Psalms. What are the main themes the Holy Spirit has been impressing on your heart? Ask God whether you're ready to press on, or whether you'd benefit more from going back to something you've already covered to take more time to drink it in. There's no rush! Remember your goal: to see the world increasingly from God's perspective. At this point, what would help you do that?

The other New Testament letters.

These are an assortment of messages from other leaders of the early church. As with Paul's letters, a little basic background is extremely helpful. As you read the following letters, listen also for echoes of other parts of the Bible. Hebrews contrasts the New Covenant with the Old. John speaks about the connection between belief, love, and obedience—you've heard that from Jesus and other biblical writers.

- Hebrews
- James
- 1 & 2 Peter
- 1, 2, & 3 John
- Jude

For each letter, write down:

- What are two or three things this writer wants me to know about God and/or Christ?
- What are two or three things this writer wants me to do in response to what I know?

Pay special attention to the links between practice and doctrine: do this *because* God has done this. If you find it hard to do automatically the things James or Peter urge, go back to the reasons they give and ask yourself, "Do I believe this in my gut?" Pray for God to enable you to *believe* in order to *do*. Make note of passages that speak to areas of your life that could use special focus.

1 & 2 Samuel.

Genesis and Exodus have introduced you to the Old Testament history that is most important to your understanding of what God has done for you in Christ. Now fast-forward a couple of centuries. The Israelites have conquered the Promised Land in part, but because of their weak faith, God has not allowed them to overcome their rivals completely. Several other ethnic groups, especially the Philistines, are still harassing the Israelite tribes. The Israelites think the problem is that they lack a human warrior-king to unify and lead the tribes in battle. God thinks the problem is that they don't take their divine King seriously enough.

First and Second Samuel tell the story of Israel's transition from a tribal confederacy to a centralized nation under a human king. The contrast between Israel's first two kings, Saul and David, is full of valuable lessons for your own character growth. But more than that, these books will help you hear Jesus' favorite phrase, "the kingdom of God," with the background His disciples had. The Messiah was the heir of David's throne—that's why you saw Him called "son of David" in the Gospels. As you read 1 and 2 Samuel, ask,

- What did God want from citizens of His kingdom?
- What did God want from leaders in His kingdom?
- What flaws in the citizens and leaders made the ethnic kingdom of Israel fall short of what God wanted?

When you've finished these books, reflect on them with Jesus in mind. What do you think the people of Jesus' day wanted the Messiah, the "son of David," to be and do? How are Jesus and His New Covenant kingdom different from those expectations? Also, think about your own life. As a citizen of the kingdom participating in a local community of believers, what can you learn from 1 and 2 Samuel about how to be a good citizen and a good leader?

Consider telling someone something you've learned. Maybe you have a co-worker who isn't a Christian. You could say, "You know, I've been reading in the Bible about two leaders, and I've learned something about leadership. . . ."

Proverbs.

Proverbs is the easiest of the Wisdom Books. Here are some questions to guide your reading:

- What is wisdom?
- How does a person get wisdom?
- What are the consequences of not taking the pursuit of wisdom seriously?

- What are some of the main areas of wise living that Proverbs addresses? (For example, money, talking, friendships.)
- What is one area in which I need to develop wisdom?

Isaiah.

Isaiah will be your taste of the Prophets. He was a statesman in Jerusalem during the reigns of several kings. For background, you might want to read 2 Kings 15–19 (note that Azariah in 2 Kings 15 is Uzziah in Isaiah 6). It's helpful to know that David's united kingdom of Israel had split into two pieces: Judah and Israel. Isaiah was in Judah.

Isaiah's book is a collection of prophecies that are not in chronological order. In any given prophecy, Isaiah sometimes switches focus from the present political situation to the distant future. That can be disorienting for you when you read his book until you get used to it. God sees all times as "now."

Isaiah addresses two main themes: *warning* about the consequences of ignoring God and the *promise* of God's future grace beyond those consequences. Look for these things:

- What does Isaiah say about God—His values, feelings, abilities, and so on?
- What glimpses of Christ and His kingdom do I see?

In Isaiah 1–12, the prophet is talking to Judah and its leaders who are trying to run their lives without God. Isaiah 13–23 is a series of prophecies against the nations surrounding Judah (read them quickly for the big picture they offer of God's character and values). Isaiah 24–35 shifts back and forth between a current political struggle and visions of Christ's kingdom. Chapters 36–38 recount a crisis when Assyria almost conquers and destroys Judah (Assyria has already destroyed the northern kingdom of Israel, and Judah is all that's left). Chapter 39 is an ominous warning that in a few decades after Isaiah's death, Babylon will overrun Assyria and become God's means of judging Judah. After chapter 39, you need to imagine a gap of more than a century. Because Judah persistently ignored God's warnings through prophets like Isaiah, God finally allowed Babylon to destroy Judah and send the people into exile. There they languished for seventy years. At last God raised up Cyrus, king of Persia, to defeat Babylon and allow a remnant of Jews to return to Judah. Isaiah 40–66 contains prophecies addressed to that remnant (who would not be born until long after Isaiah was dead).

Even if a lot of Isaiah goes over your head, try to get a picture of the God Isaiah worshiped. Is this a God who deserves your worship? What is your life like if this is the God who actually reigns over your universe now?

Revelation.

Like Isaiah, John (the author of Revelation) had glimpses of the time when God would bring His kingdom in its fullness. Both men wrote about the future in order to motivate their readers to live in the present with faith and hope. When you read Revelation, don't get derailed if you don't understand the meaning of every element (what are the four horses? who are the two witnesses?). Read for four things:

- What picture of God the Father does John give?
- What picture of Jesus Christ does John give?
- What is my ultimate future?
- How does God want His people to live now in light of that future?

Again, is this a God you can worship?

When you finish Revelation, you will have read the whole New Testament and key sections of the Old. Take some extended time to review what you've learned— a full day of solitude would be invaluable. Here are some questions to pray about:

- Who is God?
- Who am I if I am committed to this God?
- Where is my life going?
- What is my life about?
- What does my world look like from God's point of view?
- What priorities is the Holy Spirit calling me to for the next year?

Notes

The Big Picture

1. A. W. Tozer, *That Incredible Christian* (Camp Hill, Penn.: Christian Publications, Inc.), quoted in "Reflections," *Christianity Today* (April 28, 1997), Vol. 41, No. 5, p. 70.
2. Walt Russell, *Playing With Fire* (Colorado Springs: NavPress, 2000), p. 26.
3. Dallas Willard, *The Divine Conspiracy* (New York: HarperCollins, 1998), pp. 337-338.
4. This is said not to dismiss anything we might learn from the Bible about physics, biology, or the humans in the various narratives. It is said to focus you on what is most important: God Himself.
5. Phillip Pullman, *The Amber Spyglass* (New York: Knopf, 2000).

The Warranty

1. Tom Minnery, *Focus on the Family Citizen* (June 23, 1997); quoted in "Reflections," *Christianity Today* (October 6, 1997), Vol. 41, No. 11, p. 70.
2. Dates are from Tremper Longman, *Reading the Bible with Heart and Mind* (Colorado Springs: NavPress, 1997), p. 73. Because the biblical books don't come with dates and not all the authors are identified by name, scholars debate the dates.

3. Longman, p. 73.

4. David Crabtree, J. A. Crabtree, and Ron Julian, *The Language of God: A Commonsense Approach to Understanding and Applying the Bible* (Colorado Springs: NavPress, to be published in Fall, 2001).

5. Crabtree, Crabtree, and Julian.

6. Crabtree, Crabtree, and Julian.

7. Longman, p. 73.

8. Longman, p. 75.

9. *Baker's Evangelical Dictionary of Biblical Theology* (http://bible.crosswalk.com/Dictionaries/BakersEvangelicalDictionary/bed.cgi), "Apocrypha"; *The Catholic Encyclopedia* (http://newadvent.org/cathen/01601a.htm), "Apocrypha"; Longman, pp. 74-76.

10. Longman, p. 78.

11. Walt Russell, *Playing With Fire* (Colorado Springs: NavPress, 2000), p. 276.

12. Gordon Fee and Douglas Stuart, *How to Read the Bible for All It's Worth* (Grand Rapids: Zondervan, 1981, 1993), p. 35.

13. Herbert Lockyer, *All the Doctrines of the Bible* (Grand Rapids: Zondervan, 1964), p. 8; quoted in Longman, p. 81.

14. I am indebted to Dallas Willard for this explanation.

15. G. K. Chesterton, *William Blake*; quoted in *The Quotable Chesterton: A Topical Compilation of the Wit, Wisdom and Satire of G. K. Chesterton* (San Francisco: Ignatius, 1986) p. 63.

The Transformed Life

1. John Stott, *Authentic Christianity*; quoted in "Reflections," *Christianity Today* (September 6, 1999), Vol. 43, No. 10, p. 104.

2. Susan C. Vaughn, M.D., *The Talking Cure: The Science Behind Psychotherapy* (New York: Grosset/Putnam, 1997) pp. 16-35.

3. Dallas Willard, *The Divine Conspiracy* (New York: HarperCollins, 1998), p. 112.

4. Jim Petersen, *Lifestyle Discipleship* (Colorado Springs: NavPress, 1993), pp. 105-113.

5. Petersen, p. 109.

6. Willard, p. 325.
7. Walt Russell, *Playing With Fire* (Colorado Springs: NavPress, 2000), p. 89.
8. Russell, pp. 88-89.
9. Russell, pp. 95-96.
10. Russell, p. 95.
11. Adapted from Dallas Willard, *Hearing God* (Downers Grove: InterVarsity, 1984, 1993, 1999), pp. 161-164. Madame Guyon's book was originally entitled *Short and Very Easy Way of Prayer*. It has been published in English with some modifications as *Experiencing the Depths of Jesus Christ*.
12. Willard, *The Divine Conspiracy*, pp. 362-363.
13. David Crabtree, J. A. Crabtree, and Ron Julian, *The Language of God: A Commonsense Approach to Understanding and Applying the Bible* (Colorado Springs: NavPress, to be published in Fall, 2001).
14. Crabtree, Crabtree, and Julian.
15. Crabtree, Crabtree, and Julian.
16. Crabtree, Crabtree, and Julian.
17. Crabtree, Crabtree, and Julian.
18. Russell, p. 68.
19. To see many of these clues applied to specific passages, see Merilyn J. MacLeod and Mim Pain, *Jesus' Farewell Teachings* (Colorado Springs: NavPress, 1996) p. 69.
20. Adapted from Crabtree, Crabtree, and Julian.
21. Russell, p. 38.
22. Philip Yancey, *A Guided Tour of the Bible* (Grand Rapids: Zondervan, 1989), p. 13.
23. Crabtree, Crabtree, and Julian.
24. Crabtree, Crabtree, and Julian.
25. Crabtree, Crabtree, and Julian.
26. Crabtree, Crabtree, and Julian.
27. Crabtree, Crabtree, and Julian.
28. Crabtree, Crabtree, and Julian.
29. *The American Heritage Dictionary of the English Language* (Boston: Houghton Mifflin, 1976), p. 1118.

30. J. D. Douglas and Merrill C. Tenney, editors, *The New International Dictionary of the Bible* (Grand Rapids: Zondervan, 1987), p. 863.
31. Crabtree, Crabtree, and Julian.
32. Crabtree, Crabtree, and Julian.
33. Crabtree, Crabtree, and Julian.
34. Crabtree, Crabtree, and Julian.
35. Crabtree, Crabtree, and Julian.

The Parts

1. Martin Buber, *The Five Books of Moses;* quoted in *Christianity Today* (August 11, 1997), Vol. 41, No. 9, p. 40.
2. Literal Hebrew, see NASB marginal note.
3. Adapted from Dallas Willard, *Hearing God* (Downers Grove: InterVarsity, 1984, 1993, 1999), p. 35.
4. Many scholars prefer to refer to "narrative" rather than "story" in the Old Testament because "story" suggests fiction to some people. Because "narrative" has a technical ring to it, this book will often refer to Old Testament "stories." This term should not be interpreted as casting doubt on the historical accuracy of the narratives.
5. Walt Russell, *Playing With Fire* (Colorado Springs: NavPress, 2000), p. 102-104.
6. Gordon Fee and Douglas Stuart, *How to Read the Bible for All It's Worth* (Grand Rapids: Zondervan, 1981, 1993), p. 79.
7. David Crabtree, J. A. Crabtree, and Ron Julian, *The Language of God: A Commonsense Approach to Understanding and Applying the Bible* (Colorado Springs: NavPress, 2001).
8. Russell, p. 120.
9. Fee and Stuart, p. 206.
10. Russell, p. 161.
11. Fee and Stuart, p. 166.
12. Russell, pp. 199-200.

13. Dallas Willard, *The Divine Conspiracy* (New York: HarperCollins, 1998), p. 334.
14. Russell, p. 217.
15. Willard, *The Divine Conspiracy*, p. 336.
16. Russell, p. 252.

A Plan

1. Edmund P. Clowney, *Tabletalk* (March 1995); quoted in "Reflections," *Christianity Today* (April 27, 1998), Vol. 42, No. 5, p. 93.

Author

Former senior editor of Bible studies at NavPress and author of more than fifty study guides, **Karen Lee-Thorp** has spent almost two decades exploring how people grow spiritually. Her books include *A Compact Guide to the Christian Life, How to Ask Great Questions,* and *Why Beauty Matters.* She was the series editor for the LifeChange Bible study series. A graduate of Yale University, she speaks to women's groups and writes from her home in Brea, California.

QUICK, EASY TOOLS FOR FINDING THE INFORMATION YOU NEED.

A Compact Guide to Discovering God's Will

All of us face a major issue at some point in our lives, whether it be career selection, choice of college, or who to marry. Learn to listen to God and make choices that honor Him.

A Compact Guide to Discovering God's Will (Gordon S. Jackson) $9

A Compact Guide to the Christian Life

A Compact Guide to the Christian Life is an instant source of information on the Christian faith and how it applies to life in the modern world. Explore topics such as prayer, starting a small group, friendship, marriage, money, and much more!

A Compact Guide to the Christian Life (Karen Lee-Thorp) $9

A Compact Guide to Balancing Your Life

This compact guide's reader-friendly format leads you to ideas, tips, and biblical insights of what a balanced life looks like—a balanced life with God in control!

A Compact Guide to Balancing Your Life (Brad Lewis) $9